Back on TRACK

Matthew Burton

**Illustrations by
Chris Madden**

wron

First published in Great Britain in 2021 by Wren & Rook

ISBN: 978 1 5263 6406 7
E-book ISBN: 978 1 5263 6407 4

10 9 8 7 6 5 4 3 2 1

MIX
Paper from
responsible sources
FSC® C104740

Wren & Rook
An imprint of
Hachette Children's Group
Part of Hodder & Stoughton
Carmelite House
50 Victoria Embankment
London EC4Y 0DZ

An Hachette UK Company
www.hachette.co.uk
www.hachettechildrens.co.uk

Editorial Director: Laura Horsley
Senior Editor: Sadie Smith
Art Director: Laura Hambleton
Designed by Claire Yeo

Printed in the United Kingdom

The webs_____d at
the time o_____s or
addresse_____ok.
No respo_____ther
_____

For our beautiful Margot Daisy Burton, who we're so happy to meet ... and for the brilliant Gwen Burton, my lovely Nana, who we have missed dearly for a year we won't get back.

You might have been born 97 years apart, but you're both our inspirations.

CONTENTS

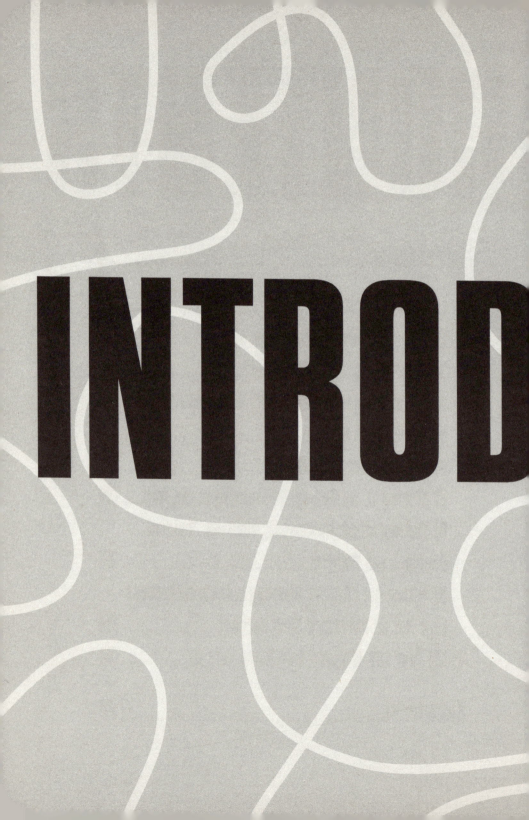

When things are tough, it can often be really hard to see how things are going to get better. You get stuck in a rut, negative feelings creep in and, all of a sudden, you lose all motivation. It's very easy to feel like you're the only person who's feeling like you do. Well, it's important to remember this:

you are NOT alone.

There are millions of people who feel just like you do.

Now, I'm not a detective or a clairvoyant, but I imagine you're reading this book because you're at secondary school. You've probably settled in, made some friends and you know the subjects you like and the ones you loathe. But, not only that, added to all the usual chaos that's involved with growing up and progressing through secondary school, you've just managed to survive the most **BONKERS** few years ever – a pandemic, no school, exam chaos – *whhhhaaaat?!*

So, let me guess[1] – you're feeling a little bit ... frazzled? A bit dazed? A bit like that moment when you're comfortably asleep and your mum turns the light on and shouts,

COME ON, TIME TO GET UP!

Like you can't be bothered? Like everything – even those things that six months ago you used to love doing – is just **pointless**?

Well, don't worry. Really, don't. We all feel that way sometimes and all these feelings are normal.

[1] And I *promise* I'm not a mind-reader either.

But there are things you can do to build your confidence, get back your mojo, find a bit of hope, turn that frown firmly upside down and get back on track.

That's why I've written this book.

Is it going to give you all the answers about school? No, that would be cheating.

Is it (hopefully) going to be your (sometimes) go-to guide if you need a little bit of help (from a book, not a real person).[2] I hope so. I really, really hope so.

(real person) →

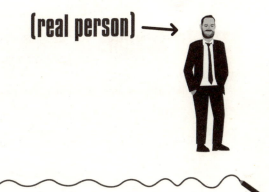

---

[2] Although I am actually a real person. Nip me – go on. OUCH, you SWINE! See?!

ME AND YOU

If I were you, I'd be asking what my qualifications are to be giving these hints and tips. We've already identified that I'm not a clairvoyant or a detective, but I am a head teacher. It's a job that's busy, and happy, and sad, and tough, and amazing, and exhausting, and the day can go from walking into a maths lesson and finding out an entire class have just absolutely *smashed* their mock exams to consoling a crying student in the canteen within two minutes. In fact, it's not a million miles from your experiences of school!

I spent my time at school in the 1700s[3] and went through primary school, secondary school, sixth form and then university. It was at that point I thought long and hard about what I wanted to do ...

and I decided to go back to school.

Not to finish any exams or pick up my school bag that I'd left there hundreds of years ago, but to become a teacher. You might know this from another book, *Go Big*, that I wrote

[3] Actually, not *quite* then, but it was *before* the internet and mobile phones were actual things.

about the jump from primary to secondary school, and if so, I'm really sorry for banging on about me again. Because this is about you. Yes,

Problems. Issues. Bumps and holes in the road. Nightmares. Catastrophes. Days to write off. Days you just want to wake up, go back to bed and wake up the day after. Whatever you call them, we all have them. And **SLAP BANG** in the middle of secondary school – with pressures mounting, growing up, growing pains, puberty, rising anxiety about the future, pressure to go and grab those grades, stressing about what's next in your big life plan – those problems can sometimes feel like they're out to get you, drag you down under the surface and drown you.

Talking about them is hard, and admitting you're struggling is even harder.

[4] Who, me?! Yes, you!

Working in a school in my various jobs, I've seen *so many people* go through this –

every single one of them feeling like they're the only one

– and one of the things I've learnt is that experience of helping people goes a long way. As a teacher, the more you hear, the more you know ... so I've pulled some of those bits and pieces of advice together in this lovely book[5] and I hope that it'll help you when you find yourself looking for solutions.

[5] With those *lovely* curved corners – aren't they nice?!

LOOKING FORWARD WITH HOPE

On top of all the normal ups and downs,

you've just gone through the **CRAZIEST** few years imaginable.

Since 2020 started, COVID-19 has taken over our lives. Families have lost loved ones, crucial years have been missed, exams have been cancelled, holidays postponed, classrooms closed, laptops opened, internet connections stretched and strained, tears shed, confusion has reigned.

Life (as we all used to know it) changed.

As I'm writing this now, it's a year since a lot of students around the world were told to leave school and work from home so that we could stop the virus spreading and help keep everyone safe. Schools around the globe scrambled to make sure their students could learn remotely, continue to work hard, and continue to make the progress they deserve to.

Whatever your experience,

it's been hard.

On all of us. And don't think you're not allowed to feel sad, weird and a bit bruised by it all. You are. Headaches from screen time, PE workouts in front of the TV, walk after walk after walk, Wednesdays feeling like Sundays and weekends not being decipherable from weekdays.

But we got through it, didn't we?

We're here, and we have a beautiful world to look at and enjoy. While we won't forget it – and shouldn't forget it – now it's time to look towards the future with hope.

Something that felt so far away just a short time ago.

Our job is to do our bit to make sure that this wonderful world is as bright, beautiful, hilarious, fun, shining, shimmering and splendid[6] as it can be. And we have to remember what happened, and do everything we can to be brave, full of love, laughter, happiness and hope, and to make our journeys successful ones, while we help those people around us on their own way.

[6] Yes, it's from *Aladdin*. But *what a song*!

Can I be honest with you? School isn't going to be brilliant every day. Most days will be all right. Probably about a seven out of ten. The end will be lovely (a bright August afternoon high-fiving and celebrating with your friends), as will loads of times in the middle (cool teachers who help you out, lessons you'll enjoy, people who just 'get' you, smashing your homework), but the next day could be diabolololololololical.[7] You've heard of a rollercoaster? Course you have. Well, school's one of those (see below).

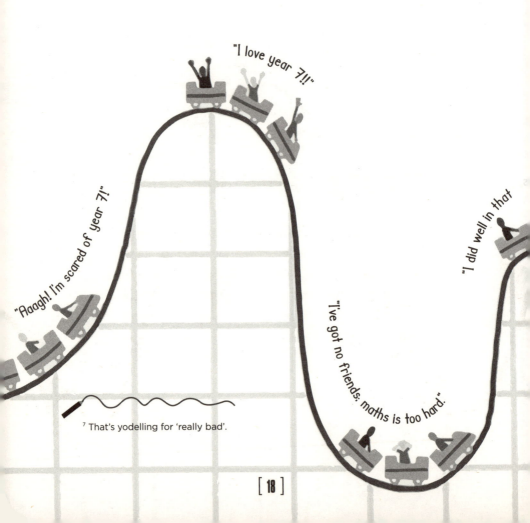

"I love year 7!!"

"Aaagh! I'm scared of year 7!"

"I've got no friends: maths is too hard."

"I did well in that."

7 That's yodelling for 'really bad'.

Most days, it's quite banal, and if, at the end of your time in school, I asked you to tell me one memory from every day, you wouldn't be able to. It's a beautiful patchwork quilt of those searing, vivid memories you will never forget – for good and bad reasons – stitched together by yawns, frustrations, laughter, tears, smiles, emotions, hot days, cold days, decisions, friendships, fallouts, boyfriends, girlfriends and family.

"Je suis un French speaker extraordinaire!"

ssignment!"

"I don't want to do French for GCSE."

"Oh no. Exams."

But it's also a road that takes you on a journey from place A to place B – your destination. With 'A' being the 11-year-old little cherub with a smiley face, who is

SO ENTHUSIASTIC ABOUT SCHOOL THAT I COULD BURST AT ANY MOMENT! OHMYGOD IS THAT A CLASSROOM? I LOVE CLASSROOMS THEY'RE SO COOL!

and 'B' the mature young adult who's making calls on their future right now, will soon legally be an adult and can vote for who they want to lead the country in two years' time. That's a big journey. And you're the one taking the trip.

So this book is here for you. For the moments of happiness, pain, sadness and worry, whether about exams, hormones, motivation, behaviour, homework, revision or things being a bit rubbish at home. It's a friendly reminder about what's important. It's a soothing bath after a long walk home in the cold.[8] It's that feeling of comfort of pulling your lovely warm uniform back on after a particularly cold lesson on the sports field. While it is still – you know – a book, meaning you can't

[8] Did you forget your bus money AGAIN?!

call for it to run over and make you feel better **RIGHT NOW**,[9] I hope it will be there for you when you need it, and will help you out of the tight spots that you will, inevitably, find yourself in.

I'm sorry to say this, ladies and gents, but ups and downs and rounds and rounds and sadness and tears and laughter and joy are how life is. And secondary school, the older you get, is like a microcosm of that. But that's for later. The things that make whatever vehicle you're travelling from A to B in keep ticking over nicely are quite simple – and I've banged on about them time and time again:

work hard and be nice.

But there are details behind those basics, and that's what this book will help you with.

LET'S GIVE IT A GO, SHALL WE?

[9] Like you could with, say, a puppy.

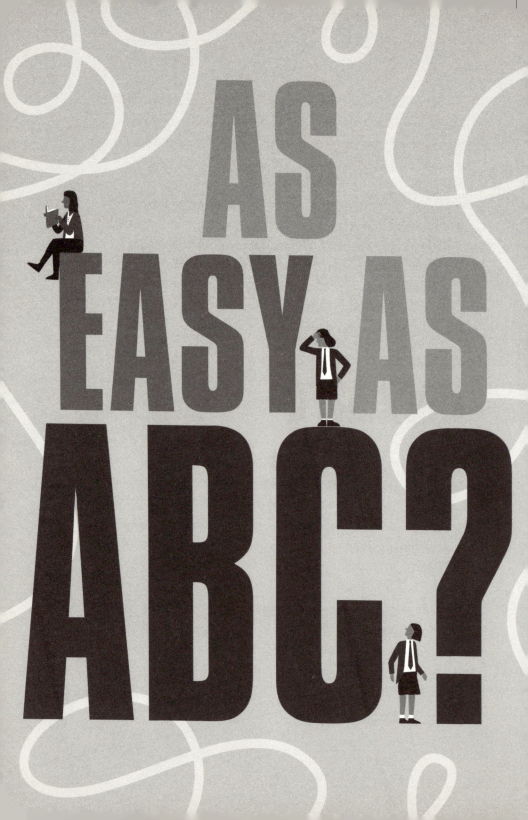

AS
EASY AS
ABC?

The 'ABC' or 'your ABCs' are one of the first things you'll learn when you arrive at primary school when you're a tiny human being with a passion for crying, messing up your clothes and missing your mouth when eating. They're part of the letters and phonics. They're important – they give you a jump-start on learning to read – and then, slowly but surely, you'll start to move on and on and quickly you'll master the alphabet. Your ABCs are the really basic things you're taught that are the foundation for a lot of the learning which will come next.

Well, while most people in secondary school won't learn their alphabet from scratch again (you've got more difficult things to think about ...), there are a new set of ABCs that you need to get your head around. If you do them well, then they're the basics that will put you on the path to being happy, successful and to making sure you get that brown envelope full of the grades you need to go on and be an astronaut, master haberdasher, mechanic, silversmith, dancer, fountain-pen fabricator, teacher or make-up artist.[1]

The very basics are what your teachers will ask you to do every day until they've run out of oxygen. They are the things

[1] Other occupations are available, and I understand that these probably make up about 0.000004% of every job going.

they'll be reciting in their sleep night after night – they're the minimum expectations of being in secondary school. 'What are they, Matthew?'[2] I hear you ask.

Well, they are:

ATTENDANCE

It should go without saying, but this is important:

TURN UP TO SCHOOL.

[2] Oi, I'm a teacher. It's 'Mr Burton'.

Unless there's a reason you can't, then get to school. If you *have* to miss something, then have a chat with your friends and teachers to see what you missed, and make sure you catch up. You don't want to miss something completely that you are going to need to know later. For example, in history, you might've missed the very first lesson on the Crusades. Now, there's a *lot* of information to learn there before you actually get to the First Crusade in 1096, and missing it isn't ideal. Imagine picking up your favourite TV series at Episode Five without the bit at the beginning which says, *'Previously on ...'* – you wouldn't be able to get your head around it so easily. If you have missed something because you were poorly, talk with your teacher and I'm sure they will make certain that you understand everything you need to before the next lesson. (See more on 'catching up' on pages 72–83.)

BEHAVIOUR

Another one that might sound easy, and you could be thinking, 'How on **EARTH** is this clown filling a book with this? I know I have to behave!'

I know it's simple. That's why it's in the ABC of secondary school. But it's so important. The impact of your own behaviour isn't just about *your* chances, and *your* reputation. You might know everything about every subject going and sail through school super-easily. You might be able to master complex simultaneous equations even when you've been swung around a roundabout at a ferocious pace by the World's Strongest Man after he's had a particularly muscular episode. Well done. I hope that *is* you. But that isn't everyone.

The way you act has an impact on other people. People can see your example and use it as something they should do. So make it a good example.

Do the right things.
BE KIND.

If you shout out in class, do things you shouldn't, act in a way that you *know* isn't right, then others can follow your example too. The impact of your behaviour on them *could* be massive . . . and it could have a huge impact on them and their future, too.

Also, classrooms work best when *everyone* is on a journey together. That means letting the teacher teach, and letting the students learn. If you find that you struggle with your behaviour, it's worth considering that behaviour often comes from somewhere. There might be stuff at home, worries in school, anger about the way your life is going; quite often, it turns out to be because you find the work too hard (or too easy). You can be a part of that solution by asking for some support – everyone *wants* to help, you just need to ask.

CLASSROOMS

This is your place to shine. This is where you bring it all together. The attendance (turning up) and the behaviour (tuning in) combine in here to give you the chance to perform. It's the place to do your best, learn what you need to learn, and to leave knowing more than when you arrived. Leave nothing to chance, ask every question you need to, and squeeze every bit you possibly can out of those boxy rooms full of pupils, chairs, tables and teachers. You might not think it now, but you will (probably) wish you could go back to them when you leave school![3]

ERRRRM, IS IT REALLY THAT SIMPLE?

Most of the time, yes. It's usually fairly simple. That's it. Book finished. Bye.

[3] Some people *do* go back and get a job in those places. They're called teachers. Strange people ...

ADVICE FINISHED

BOOK OVER

Only joking.

DO NOT PUT IT DOWN.

It would be fairly pointless having another 175 pages of writing if it was *so* simple *all* the time, wouldn't it? After all, this is not a leaflet; it's a book.[4]

Of course, it's important that you remember that other stuff around your school life will happen, too. For example, if I ask you now, 'What will happen in the next hour?' then you might *think* you know. You're having something to eat and you're doing your homework. Fine. That's quite likely. If we drew a probability chart, then a biiiiiig chunk of that chart would be just that: 'Having some food and doing my homework.'

Can you *definitely* guarantee that will happen, though? No. Think of a few more things that *could* happen. Think creatively. Go a bit daft. Could the light bulb in your bedroom pop, meaning you can't see your exercise book? I suppose so. Could you stub your toe on the door frame[5] chasing your brother out of your bedroom? Possibly. Could there be a power cut, meaning you can't cook dinner or do your homework on your computer? Yes. Could you fall out with a

---

[4] With lovely curved edges. Did I mention the curved edges? Oooooohhh. Lovely.
[5] Ouch. You have my sympathy.

friend over text, get a headache, trip over, get sad, or get the wrong idea about a status on social media and start worrying about it?

Yes.
DEFINITELY.

These are all very typical things which could potentially throw you ever so slightly off course, but they're not emergencies.[6] They're normal things which are part of what happens in houses everywhere, every single day. By keeping your eye on what's important – your ABC – you're doing the right things that will help you glide towards your goals with all the grace of an Olympic ice skater, even when these little annoyances come along. Because they will –

they're life!

[6] Unless your toe starts to go a funny shape and/or colour. Then get it looked at.

PROBABILITY CHART FOR THE NEXT HOUR

- Tiger arrives and eats meal
- Eat and do my homework
- Rat infestation
- Get distracted by TikTok
- Fall out with Mum
- Power cut and flail in the dark

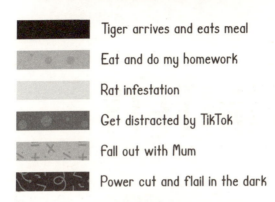

Most of the time, when we plan, things will go the way we wanted them to, and it 'goes right'. They're the moments that feel as slick as when the scissors slide easily through the wrapping paper when you're wrapping Christmas presents.[7] We don't really tend to look back at those moments in the past when we grow older. They're the ones where we're operating on autopilot. School's going fine. Home's going fine. I'm happy and so is everyone I care about.

But, despite the fact that following the ABC sounds so simple, things do go slightly wrong,[8] because *sometimes* life isn't so simple. Sometimes your brother will burst in, and it *hurts so much* when you kick the door frame chasing him out. Sometimes there *will* be a power cut. These minor obstacles that get in the way, though, won't be *allowed* to spoil the rest of your day.

We're NOT going to let them!

---

[7] You know that feeling, don't you? So slick. Sssssssssscccccccccchhhhhhh. Leaves you feeling like the king or queen of wrapping presents and looking around the room wishing someone was there to share that glorious moment with.
[8] And more about how we cope with the BIGGER PROBLEMS in detail in the next chapter.

We like having structure and even when the small things come along to change our expectations, it can bother us. Illness, injury, excitement, new friends, family problems, boredom, motivation, adolescence or happiness can all come along and knock us out of sync. That pie chart of what we expect to happen on a Monday doesn't, because something that had a 0.8 per cent chance of happening actually happens.

This can be where keeping ABC front and centre of your mind is even more important. If you think it's not worth turning up for school, that it's not a priority, then it is – **Attendance**. Maybe, right now, you think that following the rules is actually not worth it. Oh, it *definitely* is – **Behaviour**, remember? It might feel like an hour of learning about the inner workings of impressionism in art on a Thursday afternoon when you've got hay fever and your eyes are stinging is pointless. It's 100 per cent not, my friend. You guessed it – **Classrooms**. ABC – the basics of smashing secondary school.

Now, when the unexpected happens, like a car driving through a puddle and soaking you on the way to school, or realising you've forgotten your PE kit, *how* do you keep your eye on the ABC? How do you keep your focus on the things you know and the things that matter? Simple. It's who you know, how you act and how you do stuff that will help you do that. Put more simply, it's the '3 Ps': people, principles and processes.

PEOPLE

You know who they are. Friends, family, teachers. They've heard it before or they've seen it before (and even if they haven't, they'll know someone who has) and it will be *fine*. Even if you don't think it will. They'll help you. Use them. Talk to them. Let them help you out.

PRINCIPLES

What is it that you are proud of within yourself? Is it your loyalty, your friendships or your ability to make your friends laugh? Are you someone who loves to socialise with the people in your year and likes the fact that people come to you for advice? These are your values – the things you think are really important – or your principles. They're the qualities that make you, you. As you go further and further into secondary school and you slowly turn into the adult version of who you are, you'll discover more about what's meaningful to you.

Principles are SO important,

because while what you think about the world might change as you get older – experiences, relationships, exams, jobs, universities, apprenticeships, friendships, politics, *huge* life and world events will all have an effect – the way **YOU** go about treating people (usually and mainly) doesn't (or shouldn't) change. Your principles are like the frame of your bike: you can change everything around it (the handlebars, suspension forks, seat, basket, water bottle, fancy shorts you sit on it in), but the frame stays the same.

It comes down to this:

Be nice, and people will very often give you respect and kindness back.

PROCESSES

Now, I am *not* trying to pretend you are a machine in a factory churning out newspapers or plastic toys. I'm not. Honestly. You're a human being, and *not* an elf in Santa's workshop. But processes are really, really important because if you start to partly automate some bits of your day at school, and if you have a *process* to deal with the normal, usual events so they're not a shock to your system every day, then you're already winning. These can work both in and out of lessons, too. Before you've even arrived, have a process for packing your school bag – mentally go through your timetable in your head and check you've got all the equipment you'll need for that day.[9] In a lesson, when you're doing an essay in English, you'll learn the *process* of writing it.

You'll plan it, write it, and then check it.[10]

When you get home, automating the process of doing your homework straight away so it's fresh in your mind, then ticking it off your list, will help you to organise your brain ahead of tomorrow's lessons.

Aim to build a bank of processes for everyday school things – knowing the simple steps you need to take to tackle

[9] And don't you *dare* forget that PE kit!
[10] Checking is so important – you'll almost definitely find some mistakes.

how you do things like getting up, the journey to school, navigating the corridors for your routes between lessons, skim-reading a huge chunk of writing in an article you're working on in geography and remembering your passwords to get on to the computer at after-school club. This will free up enough space in your mind to be able to expect the unexpected and deal with the slice of pizza flying across the canteen at lunchtime or the dog which runs into school and charges around the playground.

And though we've already established that you're not a machine, sometimes it's helpful to think a little bit like a machine to work out how you can achieve your goals too. A process is what a machine does. It *processes* ingredients and something else comes out of the other end – the *product*. So, what is it that you want to achieve at the end of this year? Perhaps it's a great exam result or some better grades. And what do you have to put *in* to get that out? It will likely be hard work, effort and dedication going in . . . and then good work, loads of friends and happiness will, more often than not, come out of the other end and be the product of those things.

Put more specifically, if your goal, for example, is to try and master the future tense in Spanish in your second year, then it's going to need you to put in some really hard work. You know that. But let's use a highly scientific diagram to show how you're going to do it.

GOAL: MASTER THE FUTURE TENSE IN SPANISH

INPUTS

- ✴ Hard work
- ✴ Everything you've worked on before in Spanish

PROCESS

- ✴ Understand grammer
- ✴ Understand parts of speech
- ✴ Practise key vocabulary and phrases
- ✴ Master the present tense

OUTPUT

- ✴ Podrás usar con seguridad el tiempo futuro en español. ¡felicidades!"

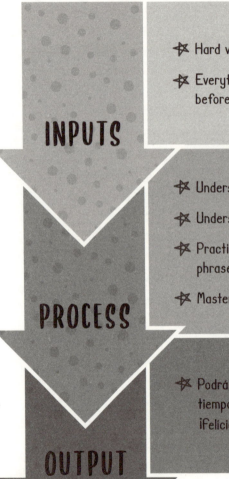

As you can see (and I hope the **VERY SCIENTIFIC AND OFFICIAL DIAGRAM HELPS**), the 'ins' are the hard work and prior learning; the 'out' is a much more sophisticated grasp of Spanish.

Finally, processes can help you to navigate those bumps in the road or the things that throw you off course from outside your lessons too, like not being in a good mood or feeling sad about something that you just can't put your finger on.

If you can't immediately work out where they're coming from, it's useful to have a **process** to sort them out, too.

Again, use the machine (the one in your head, sometimes referred to as your 'brain') and take these steps to fix things.

[11] 'You can securely use the future tense in Spanish. Congratulations!'

INPUTS

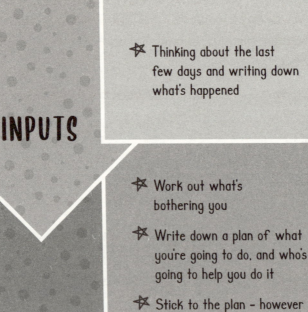

★ Thinking about the last few days and writing down what's happened

PROCESS

★ Work out what's bothering you

★ Write down a plan of what you're going to do, and who's going to help you do it

★ Stick to the plan - however hard it might be!

★ Write down how the plan went - you don't want to have to do it all again!

OUTPUT

★ Feeling much better and powering forward with your ABC!

Part of a process (especially the first time we put it into action) is evaluating it. If you can refine it and tweak it so that it works even more effectively next time, then that will be a massive help.

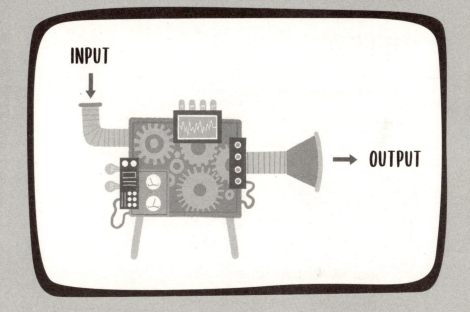

Over time, through these tweaks and minor changes, these processes will become a part of something else that's really crucial to acing those five years of secondary school:

your routine.

THE JOY OF ROUTINE

Routine may *sound* boring.[12] I would *love* to tell you that in fact its definition is:

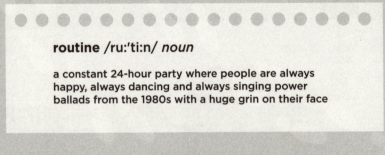

routine /ruːˈtiːn/ *noun*

a constant 24-hour party where people are always happy, always dancing and always singing power ballads from the 1980s with a huge grin on their face

Unfortunately, it's not. It looks more like this:

routine /ruːˈtiːn/ *noun*

- a usual or fixed way of doing things, *or*
- a regular series of movements or components of completing a task

So I suppose that, yes, it is a little bit boring. But putting processes together and forming a routine is the foundation upon which we build all of our successes. Whether you're that person who can turn up to a lesson, waft half an eye towards a subject and have it instantly conquered, or

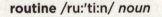

[12] It also actually sounds *really* weird if you say it over and over again really slowly – 'roouu-tiiiine, rrrrooooooo-teeeeeennn'. Strange, eh?

whether you're that person who needs to work and graft and sweat[13] and try again and again, without routines, it won't stick. Routines give us a chance to build our developing knowledge on something.

Forming a routine is about doing expected things, at expected times, to help give you the foundations to be the best person you can be. Look below:

Helen's routine

7am	Wake up
7.10am	Shower
7.20am	Clean teeth
7.30am	Put school uniform on
7.40am	Breakfast
8am	Set off to school
8.05am	Meet friends at the corner
8.20am	Arrive at school

[13] Avoiding, wherever possible, sweating directly onto your exercise book or your work. It's not much fun marking an exercise book that's wet through from sweat ...

If Helen follows that routine day in, day out, she's set for the day. She arrives on time, she's fuelled up with breakfast, she looks the part in her uniform, and she's had time to have a chinwag with her friends on the way in. Her routine gives her the best possible chance to have an 8/10 or a 9/10 day at school.

If Helen's routine wasn't followed and it looked a bit different some days, though, it could lead to some problems:

Helen's routine

7am	Alarm goes off
7.01am	Go back to sleep
8.08am	Friends call phone
8.09am	Wake up
8.10am	Press snooze
8.32am	Reluctantly get up
8.50am	Panic as the house phone goes off because school are calling
8.52am	Throw on uniform and run to school
9.10am	Arrive, having had no breakfast, sweating, and feeling like rubbish

It isn't a good start. The day is built on shaky ground and could fall down really quickly. Her friends aren't going to be too pleased because they've turned up late while worrying about her, she's in trouble for being late at school *and* at home, and her stomach is going to be rumbling all morning. We all know the luxurious feeling of the snooze button, and rolling over feeling like you'd happily sleep for the next 12 hours, but

STEP AWAY FROM THE SNOOZE!

To stop this happening Helen needs to make a plan that ensures that, on those mornings where it isn't appealing to get into school, she will blast through that alarm, say no to the snooze button, and get to school feeling calm and collected. Her morning routine needs to be so well drilled into her she could be mistaken for a high-ranking member of the military.

This plan could involve an alarm clock going off at a certain time, a cup of tea, a big breakfast, a run, a large drink of water, and a specific time you need to leave for school. By doing this and setting solid expectations, you limit the number of things that could go wrong and throw you off course.

Not all plans are amazingly wonderfully rip-roaring and fascinating.

It's fine to plan JUST to get through the day.

Planning just means you're on top of things, you've thought about what might happen and you've got the right tools to deal with the day.

So, in school, it's getting there, doing your lessons, having your breaks and getting home. When you're in your first year, things are new and shiny, and the pure excitement and adrenaline gets you through some of those more ... 'heavy' lessons and days.[14] But it's very common for those feelings of newness to slowly fade, and for you to be left in a bit of a frump, a grump or down in the dumps.

[14] Rough translation: ones you think are a bit boring.

It's the basic stuff. The grind. The grit. The getting up and facing the day. The dragging yourself out of bed even though you feel a little bit poorly. The walk through the wind in November to get to school on time. The making sure you make registration. The revision you do when your friends are going out to mess about instead. It's the stuff you do to help you get other stuff done.

The very best athletes in the world are so rigorous in their routines that those around them are in *awe* of them (though sadly I don't know that through personal experience). They work so hard on the way they eat, the discipline they show, the hours of training they put in, how they get a set amount of sleep. Olympians set their goal of being in the Olympics at least four years (often eight) before they're actually in that team. From that goal, they will train the equivalent hours of a full-time job ... but without any of the down time that non-athletes get. The processes they go through are simple, and those processes form a routine geared towards huge success. In goes the hard work, out comes the medal.

But what about when things get really challenging and, as much as you try, you can't seem to get on with school? Well, when life throws you a super-huge curveball, and you're left floundering and feel completely lost, there's another set of skills that can help you get back on track. Do you want to know what they are? Well, seeing as you've read this far, I'll share them with you.

Go on, turn the page to find out more...

STAYING ON TRACK WITH A NEW ABC

We live in a world that's anything but predictable. For a few years, most people have been waking up – at least once a month – to some news which seems **HUGE**. It might be small-huge, it might be **HUGE-HUGE**, but it can't be denied, really, that the world seems to have changed. COVID-19 didn't just tweak our routines – it turned them upside down and shook them up so much it was impossible to even remember what things looked like on a daily basis 12 months before.

And it's not just pandemics in the news, of course. There is constant, rolling coverage of all the bad things happening in the world and it'd be very easy to get a bit overwhelmed by it all. It might feel like you're walking on an icy lake, just waiting for it to quietly crack under your feet before you plunge into the freezing-cold, watery depths.

But it won't.
Know that and remember it.

That ice is usually thick, however thin the newspapers and television might make you think it is.

It would also be very easy to lose hope and faith. I would get it if young people (and that's

just to be clear) just threw their hands in the air, shrieked and ran off ... but they don't. Why don't they? Well, the more I've seen of young people dealing with utter rubbish, whether that be with themselves, their family, their local community or more widely, the more I've just wanted to stop whatever I'm doing and clap. Just loudly clap my hands, whoop and holler and scream and shout and celebrate just how *fantastic* you are. Instead of running away, hiding from the world and deciding it's far too hard to even make an effort, you just get on with it. Actually, better than that, you get *through* it.

That doesn't mean that you don't feel terrified by things. The older you get, the more you have to deal with, and having a good routine can help you with this to a certain degree. But that ice can feel very, very thin ... and occasionally it is. Whether it's at home – your parents divorcing, problems with your siblings, dealing with grief or long-term family feuds – or those huge problems that keep you awake at night – which might be climate change, pandemics, flooding or worldwide conflicts – it's often really difficult to get your head around those things.

Navigating the big stuff in life isn't always easy, and nobody expects you to be able to saunter through without needing some support.

But don't worry!

That support is at hand! There are a special set of skills we can call upon when the world cranks it up a couple of notches and really puts the pressure on us. The old ABC and the 3 Ps[1] are huge, and they underpin all of this. These aren't going anywhere, but sometimes we need to be able to shift quickly, deal with rubbish stuff that comes up and, even if everyone else around us is going crackers, keep things smooth and make sure that we don't panic. We need to show a *different* mindset and a different type of ABC – **Adaptability**, **Bravery** and **Calmness**.

[1] You remember? PEOPLE. PRINCIPLES. PROCESSES – not that I need to remind you, of course. And I'm VERY SORRY FOR SHOUTING.

ADAPTABLE

Adapting our normal daily routine doesn't mean that we throw out everything we've learned, just because something has changed. Instead we make it work in the situation we find ourselves in. If you were in a competition to bake the world's **BIGGEST** cake which required 3,000 eggs, and you realised, right at the end (when you'd spent £5,000 on ingredients) that you'd actually used 3,001 eggs, what would you do? You'd just make it work; add a bit more flour, butter and sugar, and adapt the recipe. You wouldn't start to furiously cook a pan of baked beans instead.

That would be crackers.

If you find yourself in a tough spot, wherever you can, keep doing what you're doing . . . but a tweaked version of it. So, if school's closed because of a pandemic, a snow day or because floods have turned the route to school into a river of mud and bemused farm animals are kayaking on top of cars, then get online and do your lessons there. If your mum moves from one end of the city to the other and you need to find a different way to get to school, then get those bus timetables up on your phone and set your alarm for half an hour earlier. Schools are set up to be adaptable nowadays; there are always solutions.

Find your normal in a world that's not at all normal.

Don't forget – you've already adapted once before during COVID-19 (for at least a whole year), so you've nothing to fear at al . . . just adapt and tweak.

Without this characteristic, you're a bit stuck. For many people, it is a tough one to work on. At school, many of us want things to go *just* the way we'd planned them out (and I include teachers in this, definitely, who spend *hours* every evening planning lessons) and we struggle when what we'd pictured isn't how things go. The best way to practise being adaptable is by trying to care a little bit differently. This absolutely doesn't mean caring 'less', and you should always, whatever happens, do your best. It means not being completely terrified and freezing to the spot if something that's ever so slightly outside your routine happens that you weren't expecting.

Things will, and DO, come along to challenge you and to test you.

Building up grit and resilience to smile and walk on will let you get on with your day. Having a routine provides you with a structure and means your mind expects certain things. It doesn't give you a full printout of every single tiny detail about your day to come, and your brain has got a brilliant capacity to deal with all the weird and wonderful and unexpected things a day at school will bring.

In today's ever-changing, crazy and difficult world, unfortunately, what works today won't necessarily work next week. Things change really quickly, and that thing that you spent two hours preparing for? Yeah, it was a waste of time. I am not saying don't prepare, don't plan and don't make sure you're ready for things to come along ... but what I *am* saying is be flexible and understand that *absolutely needing to know every single minute detail* of every single thing can leave you in a pickle when that thing changes with little warning.

Imagine preparing for long-distance running in PE and your only chance this year to beat the school's 25-year-old record, which you missed by one second last year. You know it's coming. You've eaten so many carbohydrates the night before that there's now a national shortage of pasta and Italy has declared a state of emergency. You've got new trainers and socks, and your PE kit is laid out in pristine condition the night before. You arrive at school. Good breakfast. Feeling good. Your routine's working well. The moment arrives – you arrive at the PE changing rooms. 'Change of plan, everyone...' calls your PE teacher. 'We're doing a different route.'

Does that mean you can't do well? No! Does it mean you're going to need to adapt your strategy so that you get things right? Absolutely, yes. You still have the tools and skills through how much you've planned ... but be ready to expect the unexpected, and you will go far.

> # Let go of needing to know every in and out of every single detail of every minute of every hour.

Wanting so much control over everything will mean that you'll be devastated when the day doesn't quite go to plan. Huge successes – just because you thought they'd go slightly differently – will feel like defeats. Go with a different mindset. Rather than thinking, 'If I do this, this, this, this and this, in exactly this order at this time, then I'll do well in my geography exam,' think, 'I'm going to do well in my geography exam, and I'm going to work hard to make sure I do.' Adapting your thinking can free your mind and make you realise that what you *thought* you couldn't do, you actually can.

Just a bit differently.

BRAVE

When you think of the word 'bravery', what pops into your mind? Is it something like a person on a **HUGE** horse, charging towards another person on a **HUGE** horse in a joust in the Middle Ages? Or a firefighter hurtling towards a blazing building with nothing but a hose of water to put it out? You might think going undercover with an organised crime ring to flush out the biggest criminals in the world is brave. Bomb-disposal expert, motorcycle daredevil, storm chaser, tiger trainer, soldier, personal assistant to a highly strung great white shark. You might think they're all brave things to do. You'd probably be right. Bravery is about doing something that carries a risk. Now, unfortunately, I've not had the good fortune to have done any of those things[2] and I salute anyone who does. But I do know that bravery runs deeper, and goes further, than just doing jobs which most people would walk away from, whatever the annual pay was.

Being brave is about facing up to something which scares you. And that could be ANYTHING.

[2] Though I did once tentatively ride a small pony for 10 metres and did mistake a dolphin for a great white shark from the beach in Los Angeles, if that counts.

Whatever you think is truly terrifying might not be scary at all to your best mate. She might think French is an absolute breeze (and she might actually really annoy you by pretending to be French when she goes from lesson to lesson, and adopting a very convincing Parisian accent). But then the opposite is true: she might *hate* the bus ride to school whereas you love tuning into your music and de-stressing from the day's hard work. Some people will be truly terrified of stepping in the school building on a daily basis, or of eating in front of other people.

The point is this:

your
fear
is valid.

Your feelings are important. Don't chuck them away and try to ignore them. Imagine if you did that with all your dirty clothes – rather than pop them in the washing basket, you just piled them up behind your bed. Pretty soon they'd start to stink and cause a problem. Ignoring your fears will cause a problem too.

Absolutely anything can come up to change things. Your plan for the day could be looking fine when you set off this morning – the bus to school, French, English, break time, history, lunchtime, PE, the bus home from school – but a phone call to say something's happened at home, tripping over and banging your head, or looking at your social media feed and getting a horrible troll's message can knock you for six and really threaten to disrupt your routine.

That's where bravery comes in. You don't need a horse and a sword (in fact, most town centres have rules making horses and swords illegal) to be brave.[3] You need to admit, understand and face what you're scared of. Bravery isn't not crying or not being upset or not acknowledging you are scared. It's writing it down, talking it through, and – even though you can't think of anything else in the world that you'd like to do less – it's getting through it, and getting it done.

☑ Turn up to that lesson.
☑ Rock that uniform.
☑ Know that everything will be okay.

[3] You also won't be allowed on the bus to school if you arrive on a horse. Or carry a sword.

It isn't doing it on your own; it's asking for help and using that help from your parents, carers, aunties, uncles, grandparents, teachers, siblings, friends or the ice-cream man (unless you have frigophobia – a fear of cold things).

Let's face it, the world's scary. Whether you're easily terrified or it takes a bit more to shake you, there's enough going on at any point to make you gulp and think, 'Crikey . . .' Don't forget – you're young, you're growing up and you're making your way.

Being afraid is very, very normal and absolutely fine.

Gritting your teeth and getting through it is hard. You might not be walking a tightrope above a tank of hangry piranhas, but you are blasting through your own fears, without a single shadow of a doubt that you can defeat them. All it takes is a bit of bravery and you will overcome (and feel so proud of yourself).

Go on – give it a go.

CALM

Caaaaaaaaaaaallllllmmmmmmmmmmm.

Say it to yourself a few times.[4]

Caaaaaaaaaaaallllllmmmmmmmmmmm.
Caaaaaaaaaaaallllllmmmmmmmmmmm.
Caaaaaaaaaaaallllllmmmmmmmmmmm.

It's quite a soothing word, isn't it? The 'mmmmmm' bit sort of vibrates on your lips a bit, and it's definitely not a word that you can **SHOUT AT THE TOP OF YOUR VOICE!**

Ploughing through school life is hard. There are so many things to do, milestones to reach, lessons to learn (both school and life). Let's not forget, that's only in the seven hours a day you're in school – there are 17 other hours which can throw things at you and expect you to just deal with them.

Either way, and whether they're actually in or out of school, there are different ways to approach these events. We all need to focus on what needs our attention (because it's important), and removing nonsense from around us is important too, because otherwise it clutters up our minds, draws away our energy from doing good stuff, and can stop

[4] Not if you're outside or on a bus or train, but if you're on your own.

us having a calm[5] focus on the bits of life that are actually going to help us learn, make progress and focus on happiness.

Quite often, when things knock people out of their routine, so that what they expected to happen doesn't actually happen, they feel anger. Sometimes it's pure anger, but sometimes it can come with an unwelcome side helping of sadness, sarcasm or sulking.

Nobody is angry for no reason.

Remember that. Everything – *everything* – comes from somewhere. Destinations are at the end of pathways – some people's paths all the way from being born to arriving at secondary school are wonderful, clear and happy; some people's are covered in obstacles, difficulties, bumps and holes in the road and huge obstructions. Anger, very often, is the product of the world cranking up the pressure on people, so that they just don't know how to deal with unexpected

[5] Remember: caaaaaaaaaaallllllmmmmmmmm. Go on, say it again.

things. Remember when we spoke about processes? When those processes don't happen as we'd expected, we can easily feel really angry about it.

People have so many different types of starts to their lives, and at the time you meet them (maybe in the hustle and bustle of the lunch queue on a particularly busy day because there's a fine lasagne cooking and your year group has been doing cross-country running in PE all morning, so you're **STARVING**), things might not get off to quite the right starting point. You might think someone's just an angry person, when actually there's a very, very good reason for their anger.

Without knowing what's going on behind their eyes, you won't necessarily know what they're upset about. And don't worry, it's not your place to go and ask. In fact, if you've just met them, they're looking forward to a lasagne and *really* don't look like someone who wants distracting from a fine Italian luncheon, I'd go as far as to say if you try to coach or mentor them to 'trust me, because I want to help you', you might well end up with béchamel sauce down your tie, an upturned pasta sheet lodged in your school bag and a helping of meaty, tomato sauce dripping down your face.[6]

They're probably not in the mood just at that point.

[6] There aren't many schools where that would be considered 'uniform', either.

Anger can come across in loads of ways – the main three ways you might express it are:

1. **AGGRESSIVE**
   Shouting, swearing, screaming, threatening or lashing out

2. **PASSIVE**
   Quietly being angry at someone and doing stuff that affects them without them knowing it's you

3. **ASSERTIVE**
   Just coming straight out with it and calmly telling someone how angry you are at them

People sometimes use the word 'trigger' to talk about that little thing that pushes them into being

ANGRY!

It could come when they're in lessons, when they're asked to do something, when they're told off about something, when they're tired, hungry, unwell or when people pick on things that they think just aren't that important.

If that's you, your teachers aren't trying to wind you up

(promise), and they don't want to make you feel that way – in fact, teachers feel really, really bad if they say or do something that makes you react in a negative way. Teachers are really self-critical. They'll stew on things. They'll think them over and over and wonder how they could've done or said something differently. They'll spend their nights frustrated and annoyed with themselves because they *know* they could've done or said that thing better.

Do they get it wrong? Sometimes. Do they mean to? Absolutely not.

Now, if that anger train is coming into the station and you feel like you're about to buy a ticket and get on board, you might be standing on the platform[7] feeling a few things. Your teeth could be grinding, you might feel hot, your body might feel super-tight or tense, your shoulders might ache from feeling so angry. More subtle things might show, too, like just feeling really, really stressed out and like you can't relax, and finding

[7] Not a real platform.

yourself thinking you can't *stand* people you actually really like and respect.

There is a way to avoid that train though. Let's call it

the ANGER Express.

The destination is *never* a nice one, there's always a delay, the air conditioning doesn't work, the toilet's blocked and you can't use it. It's a train where, even if every other seat in the carriage is free, someone will get on and take the seat *directly next to you* while hogging the armrest and spreading a laptop over your side of the table, and in that seat will be a man eating some stinking fish and slowly unwrapping an orange . . . honestly, the worst thing you can do on a train. In short, it's a journey that you'll wish you had never started, so try and get away from the station and take the path of calmness instead.

If you feel angry, try these out:

TAKE TEN DEEP BREATHS WITH YOUR EYES CLOSED
in and out, in and out, slowly does it [8]

 ## WRITE DOWN WHAT'S MAKING YOU CROSS
it might take the edge off your anger and make you realise it's not that bad

 ## TAKE A WALK
if that means asking your teacher if you can quietly step outside and take a moment, then they'll want to help you to help yourself … and if anger's something that affects you a lot, they'll know that anyway

 ## EXERCISE
a run, a bike ride, a walk or anything which gets your heart rate up and your blood flowing will help you take the focus off your anger and calm you down

---

[8] Be careful to not fall asleep …

Schools can help, too. Every single adult in that building is there for a good reason –

they want to help you.

That's why schools exist – to help. Those staff (and I say 'staff' for a really good reason, because your 'go to' guy or gal might work in Reception, might be a dinner lady, could be the caretaker, the cleaner, the deputy head, the new teacher in Spanish, the science technician and on and on and on) are there to help.

Anger's something *everyone* will feel, probably every day.[9] In some form or another, something is going to happen that's going to wind you up and make you less than impressed. That's fine. But if it starts to be something that consumes you and takes over, affecting the people around you and making you feel less like the 'you' from before, then it's important that you say something to someone. Whoever that someone is doesn't really matter too much ... as long as it's a trusted adult. There's a good chance they will know that you're struggling, but they're not going to make you feel bad even if they didn't. They'll listen, maybe make you a cup of tea, and if you want to be loud, quiet, explain in detail or just have a cry and ask for help, that's fine. If they don't have the answers, then they will at least know someone who'll know someone who will have them.

[9] Especially when you realise you've made a spelling misteak in a published book.

There are no magic wands that can be waved and can take everything away in an instant,[10] but sharing your problem can help people put in place support to get you back to focusing on what's important:

your future, and making it the very best one it can be.

So, a while ago we started out by talking about why calmness is important in these crazy times, didn't we? Well, the world is *always* a crazy, surreal, weird and wonderful place; but, let's be honest, things have really ramped up in recent times. Being in and out of school has been hard for everyone, and not quite knowing where you're going to be in a week or two has meant that planning for the future might have felt really, really difficult. Where we can adopt a calm attitude to things

[10] You are very welcome to wave a piece of wood around and see what happens, but you'll probably be better off getting that support instead.

– even though it feels like everything around us is on fire and the flames are starting to get a little bit too close for comfort – it can help us to rationalise, take a breath and do our best to march on.

The only way is FORWARD,

and no good comes from going back (unless we're learning from our mistakes).

If we can adapt, be brave and be as calm as possible, we'll navigate these tricky times and be better prepared for our future when we come out the other side. The COVID-19 pandemic was hard on everyone – a lot of people lost loved ones, missed hugs and visits to family and friends – and particularly people like you who had their schooling disrupted.

But without pressing on and moving forward, we won't be doing what we should. It is our duty to do everything we can to make sure that the future is a bright, beautiful and brave one, full of love, laughter, happiness and success. When you look back at the last few years, you'll feel much more grown-up, much wiser and ready for your next steps in life, because you can draw on your never-ending ability to apply your ABC to the world around you: being **Adaptable**, being **Brave** and staying **Calm**.

CATCHING UP … BUT WHO WITH?

3

If you've been off school, if school's been closed, or if you're going back after that long summer break,[1] there can sometimes be sentences like 'catching up' and 'making up for lost time' thrown around. You might hear them on the TV or read them in the newspapers, and your teachers might drop them into a lesson every now and then. It can easily make you panic – that's very understandable – but *really*:

DO NOT STRESS!

Now, doing a bit more work to cement your already vast and wonderful levels of knowledge is great, but, correct me if I'm wrong, I'm fairly sure that if a 400-metre race is paused at the halfway point, it's paused for everyone. When it restarts,

[1] Where your wrist hurts after writing a single word and, after one morning back, you feel like nobody's *ever* been as tired as you in their entire life.

everyone goes from where they were on the track when it was paused.

So, if that's the case then what does 'catch up' actually mean? How would you go about making sure you get the learning done from the bits you've missed, and how do you deal with the inevitable panic of feeling like the race has started and everyone else has got a head-start? The answer will depend very much on the time you've been away and what the situation is (or has been). This chapter is designed to help you stay in the calm zone even if you feel the pressure from being away, adapting your ways of working if you have to be off school, and finding those hacks to help you make sure you smash secondary school . . . even if you have missed a few days here and there.

'I'M SORRY, BUT SHE CAN'T COME IN TODAY – SHE'S JUST NOT VERY WELL . . .'

It happens to us all. The odd sick day. If you have a day off – feeling dreadful in bed with a thermometer hanging out of your mouth and Netflix on the TV – you'll usually spend most of the day feeling awfully sorry for yourself, before heroically dragging yourself off the mattress to go and tentatively pick at a meal later on in the day, declaring, 'I feel a little bit better ...' in a slightly weak voice. Your thoughts probably will, at some point, move to what you've missed at school while sweating your bodyweight out and flitting between being awake and asleep and then not knowing what time it is.

Once you've jumped off the river rapids of the school corridors and swapped them for a day in bed battling those winter bugs, jumping back into it – after however long away – can feel like a terrifying leap to make ...

even if it's just one day off.

Even after a day, your class could (but probably won't) have moved on to be doing stuff that you *just don't get*, and you can easily feel like you're in a room full of recently qualified professors of physics, nodding along with the teacher, when you've only missed one lesson and can't understand what on *EARTH* is going on.

Every cell in your body will want to panic and think you'll never understand anything ever again. However, the *worst* thing you can do is panic. You've done the right thing by giving your body time to feel better again. You felt ropey;

you did the right thing being off school. If you'd dragged yourself into school, looking half dead, fully green and feeling like you were going to vomit all over the classroom at any given moment, who would have won? Not you. Definitely not your friends (who would have picked up the bug too), and certainly not the carpet in the classroom (or the poor caretaker who'd have had to mop it up).

Of course,

attendance is important.

You know that. I know that. Everyone knows that. But if you've been poorly, or not right, or anything's happened meaning you *need* to be off school, then it's simple: you need to be off school, and that's life.

If it happens (and it will), then think about these tips that could help you to catch up and let you get up to speed with what you've missed at school:

1) ASK!

Don't be scared to ask your teachers what you've missed. They know you've been off – remember, they took the register! You don't have to tell them the ... ahem ... details of your explosive illness,[2] but they know you've been off, and they want to help you do the work you've missed. Who knows: it could be something that comes up in an exam.

2) GET THE STUFF

Lessons, believe it or not, are planned in advance. Teachers spend hours at home grafting away by candlelight at their kitchen tables with quill and ink like Charles Dickens in his prime, crafting wonderful resources and intricate plans to make sure that you can learn. The resources don't disappear, so get hold of them! Often the best way to do that is if you can . . .

[2] They *definitely* do not want to know . . . I can almost guarantee!

3) GET ONLINE!

Most schools, teachers and lessons are all set up to broadcast lessons online (as you're probably very, very aware). In some cases, if you *can* get on your lessons even though you're away, you could join the lesson from home and, while it's not the same, it is better than rewatching *another* episode of a sitcom that finished a decade ago and you've seen 30,000 times. If you're on day two of feeling rough but you can access your lessons, or at least feel like you could do it at home, then email your teacher and get what you need so you can watch and learn along with everyone else.

4) PLAY THE LONG GAME!

A few days off in March in your second year *will not* mean that your qualifications, your university place, your future career and therefore your entire life is ruined.

It just doesn't.

Teachers plan thoroughly to make sure that you get more than a few chances to cover key points, so even if you can't get hold of all the work, you'll come back to it.

5) FOREWARNED IS FOREARMED

If you and your family know you're going to be away for a fair time, for whatever reason, do make sure that you tell the lovely folks at school. They'll understand, talk it through and be flexible to make sure that, if this absence is unavoidable, then you're supported to not *need* to even think about the word 'catch up'...because you'll be able to get the work, talk to teachers and get feedback while you're away.

HOME SCHOOL

'We'll see snow sweeping across the south of the country, possibly leading to many schools closing for a couple of days...'

Even a few years ago, hearing this on the weather forecast as you thought forward to tomorrow would bring a feeling of relief and joy unlike many other feelings on Earth. 'I can lie in!'; 'I don't have to walk to school and freeze!'; 'I can go sledging instead of doing my break-time detention!' – the joys of a snow day were unmatched.

But things have CHANGED...

Schools are set up far better now to be able to deal with snow days and unexpected closures, and even though you might leave on a Tuesday and not go back until Friday,[3] they'll use their new ABC to adapt to the situation, just like you will. Their routines will be adapted so that you still get loads of the benefits of school . . . even though the building's not actually open for whatever reason.

What you are likely to need for all of these, and you've probably identified this because you're wonderfully perceptive like that, are two things: access to the internet, and a device to do your work on. If you have one already, great! If you don't, then don't worry. It's important that you get what you need, and schools up and down the land have worked incredibly hard to be able to provide them to those people who need them. Don't worry that they're going to shout at you and say,

'NO CHANCE, SUNSHINE!'

They'll do anything they can to get you exactly what you need. Can they always do it? Unfortunately not, and priority might be given to exam years and particular students, but definitely ask, and they'll be very likely to be able to help you out in some way.

---

[3] When the snow's changed into that horrible grey slush that seeps into the tiny holes in your shoes and leaves you feeling cold, wet and miserable.

'MISS, I ... ERRR ... I MEAN, "MUM"!'

As we probably all know by now, home school can be tough. Being away from your friends for a while isn't all that much fun, and sharing a kitchen table with your mum who's doing her full-time job in and among helping you to work out the meaning of the opening to *Macbeth* can be a real challenge.

What it will unquestionably do is let you see your parents in their 'work' role, and they'll see you in your 'student' role.[4] Usually that'd never happen, and parents' jobs aren't usually to be the teacher too. It can lead to stress and strain, and it's important that you cut each other some slack in those situations.

Whatever the reason for being at home and working from the kitchen table is, frustration is understandable. Of course, you'd rather be back in lessons in real life. But whether it's because school's closed for snow, if schools are closed because of lockdown,[5] or if you're off for a few days because you're not well (but are well enough to crack on with your work), understanding that things are a bit strange, considering other people's feelings, and trying to make sure that you all get some space (even if things *are* cramped)

---

[4] Possibly without those cheeky quips you make to your teachers when they're not looking ...
[5] And GOODNESS ME, we hope that *never* happens again.

by exercising outside and getting some fresh air are super-important. Your house wasn't designed to be your home, your classroom and your mum's office all at once – it was designed to be the place you spend time *away* from school and work. If that's a struggle, share your worries with those people around you. No one's asking you to be perfect, and adapting as best as you can when weirdness comes around is all that anyone would ever expect from you.

CATCHING UP

Remember, you only need to 'catch up' if you're behind someone, or behind where you should be, and even then it's absolutely impossible to catch everyone in every subject. There might be after-school clubs, tuition, Saturday school, summer school or holiday camps offered to *some* people ... but it won't be everyone, and if it's offered to you it'll be because your teachers think it'll do you loads of good.

If everyone's been away, there's not necessarily any catching up to do. If a train hasn't left the station and has been stuck there for an hour, you don't need to 'catch up' with it, do you? It hasn't gone anywhere. You'd look like a nutter tearing down a platform when the train's not even moving. If school's closed, that's not your fault. You've adapted, done your best to work from home, and you'll crack on in your lessons as soon as you can. Getting back to the original

ABC – **Attending**, **Behaving** and **Classrooms** – does most people a massive amount of good, and lets you get back to your original routine (before you had to adapt it for a pandemic, a blizzard, flooding or because your school roof blew off in a hurricane). Most people won't need anything 'extra', but if you do, then

take it and use it.

If you've only been away for a little bit of time, picking up the thread will be easily arranged. You're unlikely to be completely out of it anyway – not like when you don't watch *EastEnders* for a week while you're on holiday and you don't recognise any of the characters when you get back – and you'll re-adapt really quickly once you're back into those river rapids . . . but it's good to keep ticking over while you're at home too.

Don't panic about things if people say you're 'behind', or it's 'impossible to squeeze this in'. There is no 'missed learning', and you don't need to 'cram it in'. Your time wasn't 'lost' and you don't need to 'rapidly catch up'. There's time. You're fine.

Keep it calm, remember? Good.

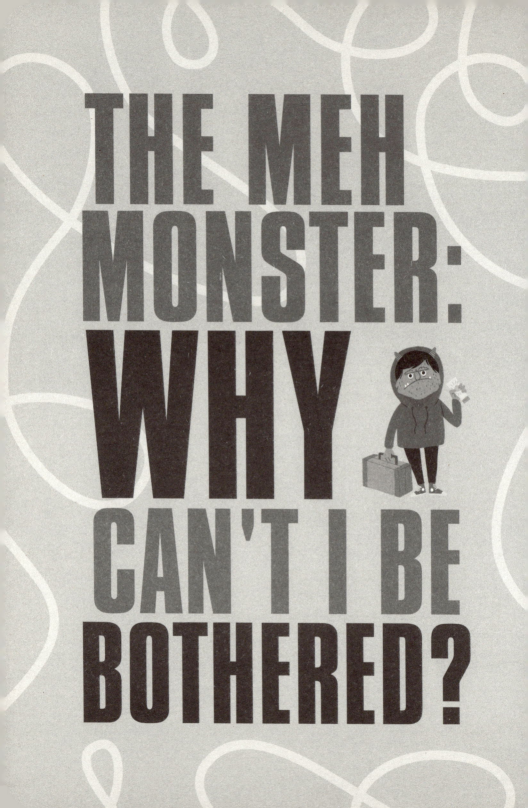

THE MEH MONSTER: WHY CAN'T I BE BOTHERED?

4

When you're at secondary school, there'll be times when you feel a certain way but just can't put your finger on exactly *why* you're feeling those things. You've tried to find something that's caused you a problem, and you've tried to plan your way out, but you *just can't find the reason*. It isn't a problem in the classroom, and it isn't anything else. You just feel 'meh' and there doesn't seem to be a proper reason why.

We've all felt meh. If it was weather, it'd be miserable, never-ending clouds. If it was a food it'd be cold, clumpy rice. If it was a colour, it'd be grey. That feeling of meh comes with its companion – the Meh Monster. It's there when you wake up, and it's often there when you go to bed unless something comes along to pull you out of it. That's just what we want to do –

find some strategies to help you see off that horned little beast with its bad attitude and stinking breath!

The Meh Monster will spend all day consuming you (if you let it), and once it's got comfortable in your fantastic mind, it'll try to build a nest and stick around. One day you could well be feeling top-of-the-world wonderful, and the next you could feel like you can't be bothered for no good reason. It can be tiring, annoying and miserable, and can slow down your progress towards what makes you happy and what you want to focus on.

It's at that point that we need to have a look to see whether the monster has moved in ... because we're going to make sure that it's not welcome here. This chapter is about spotting the signs of the rotten creature turning up with its suntan lotion and suitcases for a two-week all-inclusive stay occupying your thoughts, and then feeling empowered to turn it away before it even steps through your door.

IMPORTANT: IT'S NOT YOUR FAULT!

Don't think it's a 'bad thing' or that you're doing anything wrong if you're feeling miserable. Don't forget, you'll be stuck in the middle of a whirlwind of emotions, experiences and expectations for five years or so, and it can be (and *will* be, at times) completely overwhelming. It's very, very normal to feel, at some point, like you just can't be bothered.

Feeling meh is something that we're *all* familiar with. It's when you just can't be bothered, and everything feels like too much of an effort (including getting up on time, or going to play football after school with your mates). Despite the fact you are full of wonderful potential (and you probably know that really, most of the time, when you're not feeling meh), it's still really easy to focus on what's gone wrong and feel as if everything you do is rubbish anyway. It's easy to slip into the mindset of wondering what the point is.

Short of suggesting that you set your alarm ridiculously early, throw on your PE kit, do your warm-ups and then join me at 6am for a motivational morning exercise, a lot of the 'get up and go' at secondary school will come from one place: you. But there are plenty of people around to help, and plenty of things you can do to help yourself to find it.

SCHOOL OR SKIVE? [1]

Let's put this into a real-life situation. You have a small group of pals (or mates, or friends, or comrades, or gals and guys or whatever, frankly, you want to call them). You've been at secondary school for a year or two, and you're all struggling a little bit. It's a long eight weeks until the holidays, and you're finding it tough to even be bothered enough to lift your head

[1] Psst ... you already know the right answer!

off the pillow to drag yourself to school to do your maths assessment in the morning. You haven't revised, and you didn't get much sleep last night.

One of your friends has an idea he thinks is completely and utterly amazing. He doesn't fancy maths this morning, either. He thinks it's boring and a waste of time. He suggests to you, while you're on the way to school, that you just don't go. You'll go to the shop, then wait until his mum and dad have gone to work, and then you can go to his house, call school and pretend to be his grandma saying that you're both poorly. He thinks it's a genius idea. He looks at you, and waits for you to respond . . .

Oh no. You're NOT *actually* thinking about it . . . are you?

Yes, it'd be so easy to go with the flow, and agree – you're tired, bored of school and *really do not* fancy that maths exam either. The idea of raiding the fridge and playing games all day really, *really* appeals to you. Nobody would know, and this could be perfect.

Couldn't it?[2]

Well, no. You *know* that, really. You're aware that it's a dreadful idea, full of ridiculous pitfalls and so many things that can (and probably will) go badly, badly wrong. Skiving school because you're not motivated to do your maths exam would be a BIG mistake, and you are definitely, categorically, 100 per cent not going to do it. Let's unpick it and go through it in detail:

1) GOING TO THE SHOP

Shops are full of what? Yes, you guessed it ... shoppers. Those shoppers will see you in your school uniform and wonder why you're not in school. The people who work at the shop will also wonder the same. Not in your uniform? You won't immediately look 35 years old. People will still wonder why

[2] I know you know I'm going to say this, but yes, they would, and no it couldn't.

you're not in school (and either ask you, leading to a *very* awkward conversation), or ring the school, or even possibly ring the police to check what to do.

2) WAITING UNTIL HIS MUM AND DAD HAVE GONE TO WORK

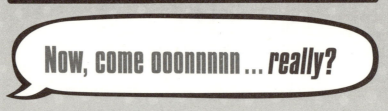

Now, come ooonnnnn ... *really?*

With the amount of nosey neighbours, doorbells with cameras in, schools with texting systems that let your parents know even if you've got a hair out of place within a nanosecond of you arriving, do you *really* think that this is going to work?

3) CALLING SCHOOL AND PRETENDING TO BE HIS GRANDMA

I'm someone who loves a creative effort. I respect a trier, and you can't be faulted for thinking outside the box to find a solution to a problem. Entrepreneurs like Bill Gates, Jeff Bezos, Oprah Winfrey and Arianna Huffington wouldn't have

moved the mountains they have done without taking a little
chance every now and then.

But pretending to be your mate's grandma on the phone to
make a dodgy excuse for not going to school is not the thing
that is going to turn you into the person seen as the world's
next great philosopher or world-renowned, highly respected
and learned scholar. Let me tell you why:

★ Trying to 'do' another person's voice under pressure
   is hard

★ Trying to not laugh while you're doing it is
   almost impossible

★ You *will* give it away

★ There's only one grandma ringing up –
   who's going to vouch for you?

The whole thing is a bad idea. At first glance, it might have
sounded easy. But would you *really* have enjoyed yourself
if you'd known just one of these things could go wrong? It
would be like playing PlayStation while sitting on a chair
on an icy lake with the sun starting to come out – how long
would you be able to keep it going before the ice cracks and
you're in *real* trouble? Probably not very long.

The other option you have, including the journey to school,
the maths exam, the tiredness, the facing up to the colossal

lack of being able to be bothered, might *sound* the more difficult ... but in reality, the repercussions of skiving off school are going to be a lot worse.

Instead, before it gets this far, you use your process: find out what's bothering you, write it down, plan how you're going to overcome it and then act on it. Have a quiet word in your friend's ear about why his plan isn't a good one. And go to school, do what you need to do, and then go home.

Not every day is one you want to write a postcard home about to talk about how amazingly inspirational it was ... but

every day *is* a step closer to being exactly who you want to be,

with the qualities and qualifications you need to have that are going to help you get there.

Knowing you've done the right thing and being able to go to bed at night relaxed, understanding that you made a good decision, is a comfort that no amount of James Bond-style ducking and diving through shops, fake grandma voices and fridge raiding can get you. School isn't a holiday – that's why the times between school terms are called 'school holidays' – but if you turn up, work hard and be nice, and keep your routines in place even when you're feeling meh, then you'll be well on track to really succeeding in school.

WHEN THE MEH FEELING TAKES HOLD

Being bothered is massive. Without that, anyone – not just you – will struggle. And it's completely understandable that anyone could lose focus at least once in **FIVE LONG YEARS** at secondary school.

One of the ways that people show they've lost focus and that their mojo has dipped is through how they act in lessons.

It could be persistently talking over the teacher, stopping others from working, distracting people, challenging things the teacher says, wandering around the classroom, shouting out, talking to people when you shouldn't, or just refusing to do the work. It might not be so obvious and you could be sitting quietly but just not doing the work and not getting everything you could from the lesson, but it could also get to the point where you stand up and leave the classroom. Whatever has happened, it's not a good position to be in. Let's see if we can put a few strategies in place to stop it happening in the first place and figure out what's really going on:

WHAT HAPPENED THIS MORNING?

Those meh mornings are usually the sorts of mornings where you drop your phone out of your blazer pocket onto the drive and smash the screen before you've even walked to the street and been met with a spray of water from the car speeding through a puddle at the side of you. It's at that point, where you're wet through, in addition to being miserable and with shards of glass tearing through the skin of your thumb from your useless phone, that you realise you've also forgotten to brush your teeth, and that if you turn around and go back to do that, you're going to be late for school.

You might have left home on an argument, after getting up late and being in a complete rush from the moment you jumped out of bed, startled, hair everywhere and wondering why you have to go to school *again*, despite it *always* going wrong.

The time before school in the morning is the foundation that your day is built on. If it doesn't start right, then the chances are that things that don't go well throughout the day are partly to do with the morning.

A vital part of that (usually before you arrive at school but not always) routine is something that many people think is a luxury, rather than a necessity:

breakfast.

Look at the word: break-**fast**. By having your breakfast – something simple like toast, cereal or a breakfast bar, even – you're giving your body the fuel to burn throughout the morning (until you hit the delights of the school canteen in a few hours' time). When you're in bed at night, you're obviously not eating, so you're *fasting*, but your body still burns energy. Waking up in the morning, you need to *break* the fast or any energy you have will quickly burn out and you can soon power down, like your phone running out of battery when it's in the middle of a messa—

Try your best to keep it calm (remember?), to leave things at home as good as they can be (although there are times when that's just not possible, and don't blame yourself for that), and to have your breakfast. If there are things going on which make that impossible, then don't try to take the burden yourself - you're not expected to - but the one thing you *can* do is be honest about it, as much as that might be difficult. Many schools have breakfast clubs so that you've got somewhere to go before the day starts to sit down, have a bite to eat and a chat, or somewhere you can do your homework in calm, quiet surroundings. Let people at school know that you're finding things hard (even if it's only every so often or it's a temporary thing) and they will help to put things in place to start making things better.

IS SOMEONE MAKING THINGS HARD FOR YOU?

The word 'bullying' can cover a huge range of things that could be going on. You might not know you're being bullied. You might not know that someone thinks you're bullying them. But it's (far too) common in the world, and schools are no different. The Meh Monster – never missing a chance to occupy someone's thoughts – will jump on this chance to suck all the motivation out of you and make you feel . . . well,

meh.

At times when life's difficult, people tend to do one of two things, and go one of two ways: they either become selfish and an even bigger part of the problem, making it worse . . . or they become even more generous and kind, and become a small part of the solution. We've all been through hard times recently, and it's so important that we try to keep positive, hopeful and be helpful, even when the news is full of sadness.

This can happen in schools, too. Tiny problems on the playground (a fallout, a cross word, a wrongly interpreted text message) can become amplified by the fact that many people are struggling with the big wide world around them, and then those people who are struggling might take it out on others. They might not mean to. There's a very good chance that they're giving themselves something to focus on rather than deal with the issues that they're feeling inside.

Being on the horrible, gross receiving end of bullying is grim, though. Feeling like you're always about to have something said or done to you, or feeling constantly affected by what's going on, is completely draining, and can make you act in a way that you usually wouldn't. A constantly churning stomach. Permanently 'bothered'. Forgetting it for the tiniest of moments before being dragged back into the misery of remembering that it's going on.

It can make you feel hopeless and lose interest in school.

Most of us will go through it (usually a little bit), but some people have it because of others picking on things about them. Their race, background, colour, size, sexuality, choice of clothes, their accent, their voice, their parents, their school bag, their home, the way they walk. It's completely awful, and just not fair.

One thing that bullying thrives on is it being kept a secret, and bullies will keep on going until someone speaks out about it. That, my friend, is the best weapon you'll have against it.

You might be in the middle of it right now, and I know it's so, so hard. But this can (and will)

feel better as soon as you tell someone.

Tomorrow, the world can look so much brighter, the walk to school can be so much more beautiful, the clouds will part and the sun will shine,[3] and because you've taken that first step, the Meh Monster will be annoyed and will start to pack its bags. Sitting there feeling completely powerless right now, without any motivation, you can't see it . . . but it *can* happen, it *will* happen, and every single human being around you who cares for you (and there are *loads* of those) can't wait to see your smile (and your mojo) come back.

There are a few lucky people (though not many) who don't ever have to put up with these things and their advice would probably be (and it's really rubbish advice because it's not advising you of anything that's at all possible) to 'just get over it'. As lovely as that would be, flicking a switch to turn off your feelings and to immediately start feeling enthusiastic about everything can't easily be done. You know how you *want* to feel (and how you don't want to feel), but pulling yourself out of the pit of that bad feeling isn't easy.

So, then, how can you feel normal again if there is no switch to turn it off with? Well, that is a

GOOD QUESTION,

[3] I can't guarantee that bit ... but you'll feel a bit more like it is at least slightly less wet and cold in the UK.

and one that, if any one person had the simple answer to, would single-handedly win the Nobel Prize for Making People Feel Better, hands down. There isn't one answer, but there are some things that can start to point you back in the right direction.

HOW TO GET YOUR MOJO BACK WHEN EVERYTHING IS A BIT MEH

1) FACE IT HEAD ON

We've established that feeling meh is pretty rubbish. It's really different to those issues that crop up, like forgetting your dinner money or your textbook, that can be fixed quickly. It's a feeling that might make you want to roll over and wrap yourself in your quilt while adopting the foetal position when you wake up feeling it ... but that's what meh is.

It's a feeling that will sap all the joy out of you.

If it's there, it's there. Get yourself downstairs, grab a slice of toast and a mochachocochini with oat milk and an extra, extra shot,[4] get yourself to school, get around people and start to think about ridding your mind of it!

2) PLAN

We've talked about planning before, but it's such an important process to go through. You'll plan all your processes as we've talked about – you know what's going in and you know what you want out – and when you feel meh, you need to stick with it and do the same. Once you've found the problem, write it down. Once it's written down, plan a strategy for what you're going to do, with whom and when, and **STICK TO IT LIKE GLUE**. The difference between planning for fixing something easy, and planning to feel less meh, is that you probably won't *want* to follow the plan for this. But you **MUST**!

3) LOOK FORWARD

We all like something to look forward to, whether it's a holiday, a day out, a new phone, a day at Grandma's house, a haircut, a day shopping, the weekend, seeing your baby sister suck on a lemon or the feeling of the sun on your face.

---

[4] AND TALK REALLY QUICKLY FOR A GOOD HALF AN HOUR AFTERWARDS BECAUSE OF THE CAFFEINE

It could be a thing rather than a time, like the sip of a Coke in the sunshine, the crunch of a really good Yorkshire pudding, or the smell of baking bread on a morning from the factory as you're walking to school.

Even though you feel like you can't be bothered right *now*, pin your mind on that thing that you love, and remember this: you're getting back there, and in a week, it'll be a week closer.

4) DO IT, EVEN IF IT DOESN'T FEEL RIGHT

The feeling of meh will stop you functioning if you let it. You'll stay in bed and just drift from sleep to nap and back again. However, not everyone else is feeling that way on the same days as you are, so loads of your friends and family and teachers will feel good, and will want you to feel good too. You might feel uncomfortable doing things, but the hold of the Meh Monster will only get stronger if you let it control you. Get out of your bed, have a shower and

LET'S GO!

5) EXERCISE

Of course, one thing on its own doesn't 'fix' it. There are no quick fixes, and there isn't a wand in the world to wave that can just make you feel better. Individually, things can help – a good bit of feedback from a teacher, a present, a lovely message from a friend – and together they are really powerful, but one thing that *really will* help you to get rid of it (even though it'll feel hard to do in the first place) is, without being rude, if you move.

I'm not bothered whether it's a walk in the fresh air, a kick-around with your friends, sprinting a half-marathon or turning yourself into a sweaty mess in a squash court. It could be racing on the back of crocodiles or doing an hour of line dancing with some older people at the community centre. Whatever it is, exercise releases endorphins – feel-good chemicals. In the process of exercising, it might hurt so much that, for a moment, you forget the meh feeling. At the end, you will feel a rush of chemicals and you

WILL FEEL BETTER FOR IT!

6) HAVE FUN!

What's better than an episode of your favourite podcast in the bath, watching your favourite football team on TV, or a cup of tea and a FaceTime with your best friend?[5] Putting the focus on doing something you *want* to do, rather than feel like you *have* to – and something that's an addition to your daily expected routine – can help you to realise that you *can* be bothered and that feeling meh *right now* doesn't define you forever. Be daft, do silly voices, jump around your bedroom and sing your favourite song.

You are a human being who deserves to be happy.

You have the motivation within you – you just need to find it again!

7) PUTTING PROBLEMS TO BED

As you fall asleep, that means the day is over. However

---

[5] Just to be clear, these are not to be done at the same time. Not only is it unsafe, but your friend will feel like they're being ignored if you're listening to a podcast and watching the football.

bad or good it was, it's put to bed, with a whole new set of opportunities and challenges to face tomorrow.

The beauty of every single day is that it's a FRESH START ...

with the added bonus that you are more knowledgeable and wise than when you woke up 24 hours ago.

There's a good chance you won't think that you learned anything from the rubbish day you might've just had, but put that idea firmly to one side. If you battled through while feeling ropey, you learned just how resilient you are. If you weren't all that motivated but still managed to learn about climate change during the Industrial Revolution, then

you're amazing.

Try, wherever possible, to not let the day before affect the day to come. Write down those problems at the end of the day in a diary or journal, and feel them flow out of your soul, into your pen and then onto the paper . . . where they'll be left. The morning after is a great chance to write the wrongs of the day before and feel less and less meh as the hours go by.

8) REPEATING POSITIVE AFFIRMATIONS

For some people, writing down good things about their life and then repeating it until it fills their mind does an amazing job of shifting the feeling on. Even if you feel that you don't have much to be thankful for, you actually do.

> You have good things in your life.

Whatever they are, write them down. When you sense that feeling creeping in, either late at night after a tough day or in the morning, remind yourself of those good things, and repeat them until you understand and believe them. Believe that you're actually a very positive person and you *can* get through this.

It all comes down to this: it can be tough to get motivated, and the overwhelming feeling of 'I just cannot be bothered!' can pounce at any point – more likely, though, when you're tired out and run down. If things are bad at the moment, and that's why you've grabbed this book off the shelf for some advice and wisdom from someone who's gone through school, come out the other side and then decided to go back to work in one, remember one thing:

it will change.

Things will look brighter and you will feel better soon.

The person who knows you best is, well, you. The best help we can give ourselves is to not give ourselves a really hard time when we make a mistake in a lesson, react in a way we later realise was wrong, or when we feel a bit rubbish and are stuck in a bit of a motivation-less rut. In fact, in those moments we need to take that time out to do something that gets us going again. Sometimes, just getting up, getting through the day and getting home is worth a reward . . . so leave that homework for an hour while you watch a well-deserved episode of your favourite TV programme.

Really (and most) importantly, if you always do your best to be kind to yourself and other people – whether you know them and like them or not – then you'll make yourself

proud.

Motivation – the thing that the Meh Monster can't stand[6] – is the fuel in the car driving you along the road through school. We know there'll be potholes in it, and bumps along the way, but doing good things, loving yourself, and treating people with kindness, definitely help you to fuel up that tank and keep that horrible feeling firmly in the rear-view mirror.

[6] Its sworn enemy until the end of time: the Superman to its Lex Luthor.

MOTIVATION
is the
enemy
of the
Meh Monster.

FITTING BACK IN

With the various stops and starts that might happen on the road through your secondary school journey, it can be tough to rediscover your place, your groove, or where you fit in. You can wave goodbye to your pals on the last day of term, the sun on your face and the world feeling wonderful ... and then wonder what on earth happened to that friendship throughout the six weeks you've been away. Often, not everything is quite as neat and tidy as we might like it to be, and slotting in and out of school is a challenge we all[1] will have to meet. Fitting in when you start is *one* thing, but fitting *back* in is something altogether different.

Coming back after being off for a while is a strange time.

It's exciting, but nervy, with a load of questions flying around your head all at once. Will I still have all my friends? Will I remember what time everything happens? Will I be able to

[1] Teachers included!

get up on time to get to school? Will the canteen still sell that exquisite flapjack? Also, the one that keeps teachers awake at night after six weeks off during the summer ... will I still be able to remember how to write properly?

It's a time where you'll feel like you're spinning lots of plates, all at the same time, worrying about one of them crashing to the ground. Now, this chapter is here to give you the tools to help you spin those plates, adapt to changing relationships, to tell you how you can ace returning to school after time off and how to fit right back in again.

(RE)DISCOVERING YOUR PLACE

So, let's start with returning to school after some time off. Firstly:

don't PANIC

– absolutely *nothing* here is going to be terrifying. There isn't one way to rediscover your place after a Christmas holiday and a whole other set of skills for coming back after a few weeks off poorly in your exam year. You're not going to go into school on Monday morning after having been away and be greeted with a brand-new uniform, a completely new building layout, and to find that your entire school now speaks a completely different language to the one they did a week ago. You probably do loads of this stuff really well already. There are some ways of helping you fit back into your role, though, that can make things much easier for you . . .

1) KEEP IN TOUCH!

Do your best, whenever you're away from school, to keep in touch with your pals. That'll make any restart feel less like forcing your feet into a completely new pair of hard school shoes[2] and more like stepping back into a familiar pair of comfortable slippers. It's great to have time apart from people during holidays, and to spend time with family and your non-school friends, but it's also good to regularly have a chat with your school crew to catch up about how they're doing, any homework you might have, and their hopes and fears for the big return.

2) KNOW WHAT'S COMING

As we know, planning and preparing is important. A really good thing to spend time doing before you return is lots of reading, chatting and preparing for that first day back. Whatever it is that's expected of you, make sure you know as much as you can about it. What lessons do you have? What time do you need to set off? What will you need to do to prepare for it the day before? Take the right books and equipment, and get your routines ready for that first day back into school mode ...

[2] Limping around screaming 'OUCH!' with HUGE blisters is no fun ...

3) IT CAN BE SCARY – THAT'S A FACT!

The first day back? Yep, you might well be nervous. You might struggle to sleep and toss and turn all night. So accept that it's fine to feel like that, and extremely normal. Also, remember that everyone else is very likely to be feeling those things, too, and even though you're panicking about what you'll talk about with the friend you haven't seen for six long weeks, that conversation will come, and I'm pretty sure you'll be wondering what you were ever nervous about!

4) PUT IT INTO CONTEXT

As I've said above, remember that not everything will have changed. In fact, it's very, very likely that hardly anything (or nothing) will have changed. In your mind, you'll be worrying about looking daft because everything will be different...

but it won't.

If you're hugely worried about going back and it's been just you who's been away for a while, it's often a good idea to

see if you can have a tour round after school one day, just to make it a bit less scary. Your school might also help you with a bit of a phased return, so you do mornings for a couple of days, building up to full days.

5) GET READY FOR THE SCARIEST PART . . .

...which is –

DUM DUM DUUUUUUUUUM!

– stepping through the front gate. Fixating on the scariness of 'going back' will often focus on **THAT** moment, when the school gate looms into view and you have to take that deep breath and big step to get yourself in. Once you're through that part, other parts of your day will slot into place, and everything that goes well will make you feel just that little bit stronger ahead of the next time you do it . . .

tomorrow!

6) FIRST IMPRESSIONS COUNT

Your first day, week or month is a fantastic chance to show everyone – yourself, your friends and your teachers – the version of you who's coming back to school this term or year. If a few things have happened in the past that weren't so good and you've done a lot of growing up and thinking, then show people you mean business on that first day ... and start to build on those positive foundations from there. If it doesn't go *perfectly*, that doesn't matter ... but try your best to start as you intend to carry on.

7) LEARN FOR NEXT TIME

Schools are always going to be very much stopping and starting. After all, every six weeks or so you'll have a week or two off for the holidays. It could be that you learn a lot from how you restart after the first holiday in your first year ... and that's a valuable lesson you're teaching yourself. Whatever you learn about how you dealt with it (and what the things that panic you about going back are), use that to help demonstrate to yourself that

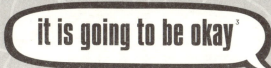

it is going to be okay[3]

and that you can, and will, do this!

[3] Because it definitely, definitely is!

DEALING WITH FALLOUTS

Next up – making friends and breaking friends! While you're at secondary school, the way you grow up can naturally lead to fallouts. It often comes from realising you're not quite the same person as when you started a certain friendship years ago (which can be made more obvious when you're away from school for a time and don't see them every single day), changes in your views of how important school is, changes in your relationships at home and, in fact, huge changes in how you see the world and what your priorities are as you grow up and school stops and starts.

Conflict doesn't always happen the 'traditional' way that you might think – with actual fights, which are absolutely horrible and definitely, 100 per cent *not* the way to sort things – but they can come from internal conflicts too. Time away from school – a summer holiday, being absent when you've had things going on at home – can lead you to be struggling with a feeling or emotion while trying to appear happy on the surface.

That's where you need to ask for help.

When you're away from school, you'll often have more time to address, or think about, those internal conflicts. You might have time to do more research, think about how you're feeling or talk to people who can help you get to the heart of a question you've been asking yourself for years. As you get older, and certainly throughout your time in secondary school, you might come across internal conflicts which change your views on aspects of your life – it could be gender, sexuality, political views, your opinion on the world or your future. That is absolutely fine. Where you need help, support, guidance, advice, a shoulder to cry on or someone to celebrate with, just know that your return to school *will* provide that advice, and those people.

They're there for YOU.

CHALLENGING OLD FRIENDSHIPS

While relationships become deeper and stronger as we get a little bit older and time goes by, conflicts between people can also appear to last longer and be more difficult to deal with. Our personalities, opinions, experiences and views on the world are more deeply rooted and we take things more seriously. So how do we navigate the challenges of keeping our old friends and slotting back into friendships, even if things have changed?

Firstly, what's important is taking an interest in people, and not thinking they're immediately wrong because their opinions don't completely and utterly match our own. There are some views that people will have that are just not acceptable, and they'll become very obvious, very quickly. Believe (because it's true) that:

1) You don't have to like everyone, and

2) You don't actually have to talk to those who you don't like

Once those facts sink in, you will feel much more free. Taking an interest doesn't mean smiling, agreeing and skipping off into a beautiful sunset together with happy music in the background at the end of *Neighbours*, and it's also *absolutely fine* to completely disagree with someone who you actually do like.

SEEING THE WORLD DIFFERENTLY

In real life, most people have good and bad bits. We're all good at some things, and less good at others. We've all done amazing things, and sometimes let ourselves down. But the main thing that we should always remember is that we are just that –

people

– and we come with all the unique daftness, wonderfulness and pitfalls that anyone does. We all come with different fingerprints, different DNA, and our journeys through life are all slightly different. That includes those young[4] people at school (including you), who are all finding their way through things.

---

[4] Young (ish). Like, not 'young' young, but not old enough to buy your own house, but certainly old enough to buy a Lego house on your own.

Now, we know we're not always going to get on with everyone, but

what we can do, now more than ever before in the world, is listen.

It's incredibly important that just because someone's views might be different, that doesn't automatically make them your mortal enemy and the vision of pure evil. It also doesn't make you an amazingly wonderful angel just because their views are different.

Debate, sharing your views, talking to other people and explaining your perspective on issues.

Whatever you want to call it, it's important. A very small minority of people just won't listen.

That's their loss, isn't it?

We all need to share our experiences and our perspectives because without that, without being exposed to others' opinions who've lived different lives to us, we'll never see anything in a different way. It isn't making you a villain to engage with someone who's got a different view; in fact, it's massively important that you do. If your *very strong* view is one thing, and someone else's *very strong* view is something else, then there probably is, in most things, some middle ground where you can find things you agree on.

That can be tough, though, because many of us don't like to challenge people – or to be challenged and have to admit that we might be wrong. Use these tips to structure debate and maybe open some doors to finding out something new about someone new:

1) WHAT ARE YOUR ARGUMENTS?

You need to have some points to make, and they can't just be things like 'Well, you're wrong, sooooo ...' Think about what it is you want to say, how you're going to say it and why.

These are important points and you are expressing your views, so do them proud.

2) WHAT ARE THEIR ARGUMENTS?

Remember, the other person might well feel *exactly* the same as you ... just with the opposite view. Think about that. It doesn't do anyone any good to stop them expressing their view. You never know;

you might
just learn
SOMETHING!

3) LISTEN!

In the heat of debate battle, it can be easy to switch into the role of a warrior looking for an opportunity to attack, rather than a considered, calm (remember, from before?) mature person who's considerate of the views of others. By listening, you're demonstrating what you'd expect from the other person, and it can help to de-escalate[5] the situation if one of you gets a bit hot under the collar!

4) BE OPEN

There's no point even trying this if you are not willing to learn. Just like you're spending time talking to them about your view, they're doing the same. The chances are that they'll say at least a couple of things that will make you think, 'Well, okay, fair enough, if you put it *that* way ...'

5) BE POLITE

Nothing other than polite, respectful conversation. You don't have to like everyone, or their views, and you might be very different from the person they are, but you will be proud of yourself for showing politeness, respect and representing your opinions with dignity and class.

[5] Chill out and calm down.

WHEN YOU'RE RESTARTING, BE TRUE TO YOU!

The most important thing is for *you* to be okay with who *you* are. There are loads of people who, throughout the ups and downs and stops and starts of secondary school (and sometimes before), might not quite feel as if they 'belong' completely to what they've always been told about who they are. That can be overwhelming, and can lead to young people worrying about what the future will be if they have to carry on doing what's always just been 'expected' of them. Don't. Ever. Think. That.

You are *you*, and that's brilliant. SIMPLE.

Part of being at secondary school is often discovering who you might be (or at least getting closer to discovering who you will be) in the future. People might come out as gay, might realise that they identify as a different gender, or could find out a million different things about their future self that they didn't know was the case. It isn't a weakness to change your view, change your mind or change anything else – life is *your* journey – and any one thing in secondary school could be the springboard to a wonderfully happy future. Coming to those realisations could also help you to understand why you feel *so much better now*, if things just haven't felt like they've quite been the right fit for a long time.

We know there'll be awkward moments where you've got it wrong. Returning after those long summer holidays can lead to friendships, fallouts and friction, and re-finding your place in your year, your class and your social group will sometimes take time. Sometimes, in fact, after a break, you might naturally change your friends – it can and does happen, and it's often after a break from the intense periods of being at school together. You'll need to re-learn about the 'new' versions of your friends and them about you from a new perspective every time you make a restart. But once things click – and that'll usually happen super-quickly – you'll be straight back to making wonderful moments where you share successes and realise that you got things right. That'll be where those friends for life who you'll grow old with will start to form, however many stops and starts happen along the way.

It'll be a lot of learning rights and wrongs and dos and don'ts, but these experiences will give you a great idea of what to expect when they occur on a bigger scale once you leave secondary school – which they will. They will help you to be able to make good choices in the future so that you make that huge **SPLASH** in the big wide world and prove that, as we knew all along,

you are amazing, fantastic, resilient, brilliant and brave.

Think ahead to the biggest break at the end of your exam year – at that point you'll be faced with the choice of just who you want to spend time with in the future both in your college, job or apprenticeship and also in your social time.

Who are those people, and what do they bring to your life?

So if you're at the gates now, wondering how you're going to get through them after you've been away for a couple of months, then do something for me.

Put this book away,[6] visualise what the end of the day's going to be like and how proud you're going to be of yourself, and take a step towards the gates.

And another one.

Then another one.

You've been here before! You've got this.

Keep on walking, and get things going again!

---

[6] In your bag, just to be clear. Please don't chuck it someone's garden ...

KEEPING
YOUR HEAD
UP ...

6

A few years ago, mental health (how you feel in your head) and physical health (how you feel in your body) were seen as very two different things and were not treated the same. They were almost like two cousins who don't see each other because they had some sort of weird argument at a Christmas party at their nan's house a few years ago – related ... but not talking. Everyone knew that they were both there, but the relationship between them was ignored quite a bit. Also, people would happily talk about their physical health until the cows came home, but if they were having any kind of problem with their mental health, they would keep all that inside. I can't understand why, really ... I mean,

IT IS ALL HEALTH, ISN'T IT?!

Well, perhaps the cousins got together over a milkshake and worked out their differences, I don't know – but over recent years, mental health has been talked about much, much more. And that, my friends, is **GREAT**! After all, if you graze your knee performing a slide tackle in the school playground, you would certainly make sure it gets treated ... and the same should be true for mental health, too. It's absolutely fine to get the help you need; it's your *health*, after all.

Sometimes we need some HELP with it.

Everyone has mental health. Let's say that first. Whatever age, whatever gender, whatever your job or your qualifications, we *all* have mental health. That includes you, in secondary school. You don't have to get a set of qualifications aged 16 in order to earn your right to have mental health. Quite the opposite – your right to your mental health is yours **RIGHT NOW!**

Mental health is often referred to when people are struggling with it. That's when they're mentally *unhealthy*, and things aren't going too well. But it's important that we remember that

your mental health can be good, too!

The ups and downs of school will lead to sometimes feeling mentally healthy, and sometimes mentally unhealthy. That rollercoaster of good and bad and happy and sad and hormones and friends and exams stretches your mind to places it probably hasn't been before (and that's before anything outside of school comes into the mix to complicate matters). But let's face up to it: you are going to feel rubbish at some points, even for a short time, while you're on your secondary school journey.

I really, really hope that you are feeling good as you're reading this right now. If you're not, though, that's fine. I hope this helps. This book can't fix it; it isn't a plaster that you can pop on a grazed knee from when your friend tripped you up on the playground (you can get them back later – grrrrr), but what I hope it *is*, is:

1) Something to let you know you're not on your own when you feel rubbish

2) Something that helps pin how you feel to something, so you can start to understand how you're feeling, why you're feeling it and (most importantly) how you can start to stop feeling it

Some people might be *feeling* like life is really, really difficult but hide it very well. They might put on a 'front', and just get on with life, appearing fine on the outside but crumbling on the inside. People deal with things differently, and if you are someone who can put it to one side while you are with friends, in lessons, or having a meal with your family at home, then that can be a good thing. But if it's still there after that, when you're in bed and staring at the ceiling worrying about things you can't control, then it's still something you would benefit from being helped with.

It's sometimes more helpful to think of mental health as being a set of scales. At one end is feeling on top of the world. The sorts of days where you feel like stuff just works. You feel good on a morning, you sail through double PE and score the winning goal, you create a critically acclaimed masterpiece in art that's picked up by the press and has sold for $4,000,000 by teatime. Everyone laughs at all your jokes all day long and your group of pals are all shining too.[1]

At the other end, though, are the other days.

[1] It's basically the sort of day where you feel like you're in a music video all day.

The DOWN days. The BAD days.

When that Meh Monster has moved in and invited its friends for a long stay and you just wonder what the point in PE and art are. It could be just a bad day, in which case a good night's sleep, some sad music and a good cry will probably make you feel better. Tomorrow you're back to your normal self. But if it's not, and it sticks around for a little while, then it could be a sign of a condition that talking to someone about would really help. Firstly in school, but maybe even your doctor or school nurse. In school, if mental health problems persist, then it tends to be linked to one of these things:

Anxiety is worrying about what might happen and overthinking seemingly very normal situations. It could come along with feeling restless, feeling dizzy and not being able to concentrate or sleep, and could be focused around being worried about one thing, or loads of different things.

Depression is a bit different. Usually it's about feeling really, really sad about things that have already happened, or feeling absolutely hopeless about the future. It could come along with feeling really low for ages on end, but can also lead to people thinking about committing suicide.[2]

It is really, really important, here, to say this: if you are feeling dreadful, have been for a long time and are worrying you'll do something to yourself which might harm you, then this book won't cut the mustard. This is about helping you before it gets to that point, so please **go and ask for help from a medical professional**. You're not weak, you are being brave by standing up to it, and you are as entitled to every bit of support just as much as everyone else. Just think about it: if you broke your ankle playing football, would you hobble around in agony for days, not mentioning it, thinking you could fix it yourself? No, you wouldn't. You would seek help from a professional, because it is the **BEST** thing to do. The same applies to your mental health.

But if you sometimes do feel these things, and they come and go like waves on a beach, then I'm sorry. That's rubbish too. Awful, hateful thought-thieves that sap the colour out

---

[2] There's LOADS more about the signs and symptoms of depression and anxiety, but they're better explained by someone face-to-face, so you know how best to handle it yourself and apply it to your own thoughts.

of your day and turn a hilarious TikTok into a boring dance. There's help for you in school. Again, approach that 'go to' person who you trust and can confide in (although it's worth pointing out that you *can* go to anyone you trust, and even if they don't have the answers, they'll know a person who does … and the least they'll be able to do is listen). Most schools, too, have someone who 'leads' on mental health, which is fantastic, and even if they're not the person you'd usually head towards, they're set up and ready to help (even if it's through someone else), either through what school can offer – maybe some counselling, coaching or mentoring – or by referring you on for some support from outside school.

Sometimes school might not feel like somewhere you want to ask for help, either. If that's the case, as well as your doctor, there are loads of resources online, phone numbers you can call, and charities who are there to help, 24 hours a day, 7 days a week, 365 days a year. And there's some at the back of this book!

You're NEVER on your own. REMEMBER THAT.

Now, if your mental health is a set of scales, then where do most days sit? Well, given that we know that every day is going to have some stuff that goes wrong, and that every day has some really fun bits, most days are going to fall somewhere in the middle. Most *people*, too, are going to fall somewhere in the middle, for most of the time. One awful, dreadful, miserable day can be down to something going wrong or the Meh Monster sniffing around ... and it's bounce-backable from, so it's not something to panic about. In the same way, if you have a day that's so amazing you feel like you could magic up a unicorn to walk you and your friends home from the school gates if you so desired, then, while that's wonderful, not every day is going to play out just like that.

Aiming for that centre point on the scales relies on you doing a few things, and the older you get, the more you're expected to do to support yourself. Most of the time, for most people, when you're a bit mentally unhealthy it will feel rubbish, but it won't be completely and utterly overwhelming, and you can help yourself through it. You won't need to get a diagnosis, or any extra help or support, and you'll roll with it. There are things you can do to try and keep the scales centred:

1) LOOK AFTER YOURSELF AND TAKE THE TIME YOU NEED

When you need a break, rather than putting the finishing touches to that piece of homework at 8pm the night before you've got a busy day the day after, have a break.

Take some exercise

– whatever form that takes – and put some distance, even for a few minutes, between your exercise books and you. A fire doesn't burn without fuel, and if you don't look after your body and your mind, you'll soon be a metaphorical pile of smoking embers.

2) EAT HEALTHILY AND DON'T SKIP MEALS!

Part of looking after your mind is, of course, looking after your body and keeping it fuelled. Sometimes that's easier said than done, and you can't decide exactly what's on the menu for school lunch, and what's available at Breakfast Club. But school dinners have to be (mostly) healthy and nutritious, and if you've got a choice in the evening, make sure you get lots of vitamins and minerals as part of your diet, as well as fruit, salad and vegetables.[3] You might love a coffee, too, but

[3] But, of course, leave a fair bit of room for ice cream. That's also important!

[139]

keep an eye on a healthy amount of caffeine, and be careful to not drink it too late, or else it could mess with your...

3) ZZZZZZZZZZZZ

Sleeeeeeeeeeeep[4] is important. If you're feeling stressed out and panicking about things, your body will need a little bit more sleep than usual. Always aim for at least nine hours and make sure that going to bed falls into your routine at a similar time, putting your phone down and leaving it, and maybe even reading a few pages of a book before you switch off the light and fall zzzzzzzzzzzzzzzzzzzzz...zzzzzzzzzzzzzzzzzzzzz...zzzzzzzzzzzzzzzz.[5]

4) KNOW YOUR CUES

Some people have certain thoughts that dominate when they're in a bad patch of their mental health. Look at what we've just spoken about – diet and sleep – and think back to the last time you were struggling. Were you struggling to get to sleep or not firing your lunch down? Also, try and remember how it felt when you're looking back after the event. You will get used to how it feels. It might start with feeling breathless, your back going warm, your palms

---

[4] NOT NOW! You're reading (and you're on a bus).
[5] WAKE UP! Your light's still on and you don't want to get night-time dribble down the curves of the book.

sweating or feeling sick ... but if you know the pattern of where your thoughts lead from when you can feel those triggers coming (those things that set you off) and you can see them happening ...

then you're already **ahead** of it!

5) BREATHE

Given that all life needs to do this to exist, I know that you know this. You have to do the normal breathing, but putting a focus on your breathing, and counting breaths in ... and out ... and in ... and out ... a few times every day can help to get oxygen into your body, distract you from what you're worried about, and help lift the gloom.

6) GRAB IT, GET IT AND GO

Every experience we go through has the possibility to make the future better not just for us, but those people who we affect around us. It might be rubbish now. It might feel like things won't get better. But they *will*. See this as a learning opportunity, and while it is painful to have to go through tough times to learn more about ourselves, you'll learn a lot about the people who help you out, the best people to go to, the things that work for you, and the impact that things have on you. Write them down on bits of paper, store them up, and when you need them again, pull them out and read them as part of your routine. You can believe those bits of paper, because they are based on your own experiences of navigating tough times.

7) COUNT

No, don't summon a vampire from the ruins of a Romanian castle, but just focus on counting. One, two, three, four, five, six, seven, eight, nine, ten. Do it again. Focus on the numbers, and take the focus off your worries.

8) REMEMBER THE GOOD BITS

Those amazing days where the sun is shining and life is so good are worth remembering too. Note them down, take pictures (to put in your box of positive affirmations) and remember that they're happening because you're you, you have those people around you, and you've made them happen. If it's dark and raining and rubbish today, take a look at that picture – it *will* come back.

9) LAUGH

Just to be clear, I don't mean in a toilet cubicle on the maths floor on your own, or in the middle of a 3,000-person assembly commemorating the opening of your school 250 years ago.

LAUGHTER is good for you,

though. A joke from a friend, or a quip from a teacher, can do you more good than just giving you a line that you can use at the family Christmas dinner table. It can help to release happy hormones (endorphins), it fills up your lungs with loads of oxygen and makes your organs do a little dance in your body. Muhahahahahahahahahahaha!

10) LET IT GO

I know what you're thinking, but I'm not suggesting that. Turning up to school dressed as a Disney princess isn't going to give you any less to worry about, so that is *not* what I'm advising. Rather, just understand that you have to let things go. You *can't* have all the answers, you *can't* affect some things, and however much you worry about something, it doesn't affect the outcome. What does affect it are the actions you put into fixing it, and you're in the best place to do that if you're free of wasteful, irritating worry.

Mental health is a massive part of your secondary school journey, and keeping it in your thoughts is really important. It doesn't have to be all you think about all the time (and shouldn't be – you've got plenty of other stuff to be getting on with), but keeping your mind healthy and on top of the many weird and wonderful challenges you'll face will do you so much good. There are pressures on you during school that you'll be going through for the very first time in your life (but ones that you will go through again) and often, because it is the first time, it can be more difficult to work through than it ever will be again.

You'll develop your own strategies, tips and hacks so that things that might trouble you now will be a breeze when you hit exam year. That doesn't mean that it's not okay to feel sad or upset – it's very, very normal – but it's about doing the bits and pieces above, and keeping an eye on your friends and classmates, too.

In fact, given that it's often the fact that we end up working extra-hard in secondary school (so much learning about subjects and life to do in such a small amount of time) to keep up with the pace of those relentless five years, it's extra-important to make sure that we keep beautifully balanced in the middle of those scales as best as we can, for as long as we can. The scales will, at various points, tip this way and that (for *all* of us, I promise), but when you're weighed down on the wrong side, shout for help . . . and the gang will come running.

People care. Don't forget that. Use them.

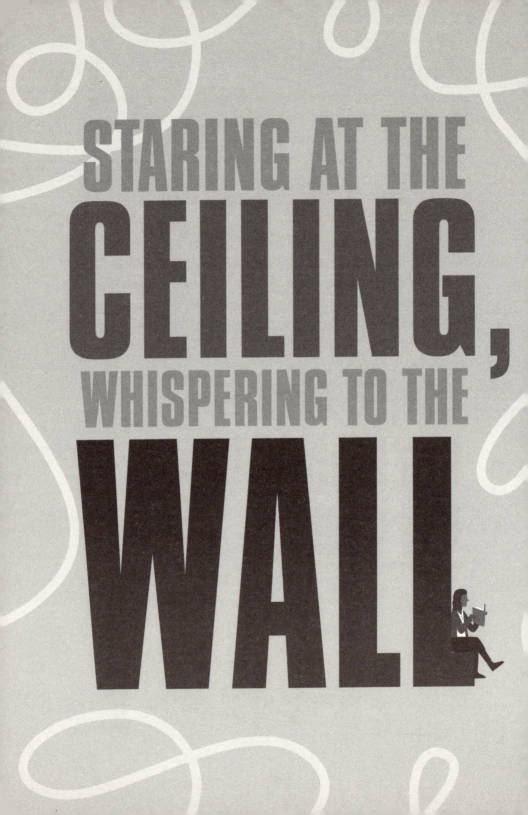

STARING AT THE CEILING, WHISPERING TO THE WALL.

7

We've focused on our mental health and what's going on inside our heads. But what about problems in the wider world – ones that might feel harder to influence or change? I believe that everyone starts out wanting to do their best to help everyone else and start making the world a better place. Sometimes, though, issues pop up along the way that aren't so easy to fix. These are the ones that keep us awake at night, staring at the ceiling until it's long past midnight, and the sorts of things that flash past our eyes even once we've dropped off, so we're whispering at the wall in our broken sleep.

PROBLEMS WITHOUT SOLUTIONS

There are some really **BIG** problems in the world that we all want to solve, but it's easy to feel helpless about them. This chapter is all about those problems that are too big to fix alone, and how, sometimes,

we have to let them go.

You can definitely do your little bit to shift them, millimetre by millimetre, in the right direction, but you can't do it alone.

Through the work you'll do in school, watching the news, reading newspapers, social media and more exposure to a more diverse range of voices, you'll see things that inspire you and make you overjoyed … but you'll also see and hear things that break your heart.

Those things that you *just can't fix*, just aren't fixable by one person. Whether it's climate change, famine, war, terrorism, bigotry (picking on people because of their appearance, belief, gender, sexuality, religion, culture, nationality or anything else). Every single one of us (me included, and I'm sure everyone you know) would *love* to rid the world of all of them with a wave of a wand. But, as much as that is the case, that just won't happen.

These problems are called 'wicked problems'. Not because they're dreamt up by a witch with a cauldron, cackling about how wonderfully wicked and evil she is, but because a 'wicked' problem is something that is an issue that is so messy, interconnected and deep-rooted that it looks, on the surface, absolutely impossible to fix. I suppose it's the type of problem that a wicked witch would come up with, if she could ...[1]

They can pop into your head from something you've seen during the day – maybe a friend being picked on for something, someone in your class who didn't have any breakfast or money for lunch and was hungry all day, a social media post you've seen which has made you feel

really, really sad.

To start with, you'll fix your mind on what you can do to solve that one thing ... but you can quickly unravel it and realise it's one problem you've seen which is a part of a much bigger and wider problem in the world.

[1] So, yeah, keep her in mind. Rubbing her hands together in wicked glee, while her lime-green cauldron bubbles away and a toad jumps out of her pocket. Eeeugh. Gulp.

FORGET, OR FIGHT?

You've got two choices at this point. Forget it, or fight it.[2] Most people can't forget it. If you're reading this chapter, then that tells me that you are, almost certainly, someone who can't just forget it. It's bothered you. It's irritated you, like an itch on your back your fingers just can't reach.

If you've resolved that you're going to fight, then doing it in the right way is super-important. Super-super-important, in fact.[3]

Fighting in the wrong way can make things much worse, VERY QUICKLY.

You might feel like wading into school wearing a full suit of armour tomorrow on a strapping, muscular horse and declaring war on the boy who made a racist comment to someone online last night. You might want to spend every penny you have buying someone food vouchers so you know they've got enough money to eat over the weekend. You

---

[2] NOT A FIGHT WITH PUNCHES AND KICKS AND ALL THAT VIOLENCE. THAT NEVER, EVER WORKS. OKAY? Good!
[3] It's important. Okay? Got that? Good!

possibly feel like setting up an anonymous email account and sending abuse to someone to make them feel like they made you feel. You potentially even feel so, so angry that you can only see violence as the answer. One thing to always remember: however big, however nasty, however impossible and unpleasant it might be,

violence is not the answer.

Hurting someone else, or putting yourself in any kind of risk is not something you should be doing, so just, please, don't. Ever. Keep yourself safe.[4]

At this point, do this for me (and, more importantly, for yourself): think. Think of what you want, and how you're going to achieve that outcome. I can't promise you *will* get it – whether it's punishment for someone, an apology, someone to completely change who they are and how they do things – but having a goal in mind is important.

[4] We'd all like to think that we're James (or Jane) Bond … but we're not. Just like I can't scale a skyscraper using no safety rope and avoid a plethora of wrong 'uns throwing rocks at me and shooting at me, neither can you. So be safe.

While it certainly is not going to fix itself, and the wicked problem it represents isn't going to go away through whatever individual action you take, you can do your bit. You can move the whole world a tiny bit closer to solving that problem by making just one person realise that they're not alone, that someone cares, and that someone's standing up for what's right. Your actions, if they're coming from the right place and with altruistic intentions,[5] are doing a really amazing thing. Pretty phenomenal, eh? So because it's that phenomenal, and because it's so important, let's plan it out and execute it properly, shall we?

1) THINK BEFORE YOU ACT

Like we've said, doing something just because it feels right in a moment doesn't turn out right very often. Confronting someone on a corridor and shouting at them won't help. Your job here is to think about what will actually solve it, and consider the right way to make a tiny dent in that wicked problem you're working against. A rash decision will often make you wince shortly afterwards ...

and there's no going back once you've acted.

[5] Doing something which is completely for someone else's benefit. So, in reality, it's not altruistic if you give someone who's hungry some money for a meal and then bang on about it on social media for the next couple of weeks.

2) START A CONVERSATION; BUILD MOMENTUM!

Whatever your plan, communicate. That means starting a conversation and talking to people at school about it – your teacher, your head of year, having a meeting with your head teacher. You might be complaining about someone's actions (if someone's done something nasty, like bullying another person), or you might be trying to highlight a wider issue (like some children going hungry and without breakfast), so communication is key here. Take people on the journey with you. Your head teacher might not even know that things are a problem – even teachers rely on information being passed on – and will *definitely* want to help.

They might suggest a Breakfast Club, they might back a campaign to make sure everyone has access to free sanitary products, or they might get behind your plan for a lunchtime march to make a point about global warming. Be prepared to speak with integrity and passion, and be ready to ask, and answer, questions … politely.

But what if it's something about the wider world that your teachers can't have a direct impact on? You could reach out further to online organisations and societies, and join campaigns which fight for your cause![6]

---

[6] Just make sure that they're legitimate and check them out first. There are thousands of websites out there … but taking information from the right ones is important. Ask an adult to help you dig out the ones to trust!

3) BE PROUD

Honestly, people at home and school will be amazingly proud of you for seeing something and acting in the right way. If you've changed something at school, you might even get some interest from the local newspaper or get mentioned in the school newsletter. Be proud of yourself and don't shy away now –

you've earned it!

That isn't shouting about how amazing you are just for the sake of it; it's being proud of yourself for doing something positive in the world.

4) BE PREPARED (FOR IT TO GO WRONG)

In life, when we try to do the right thing, sometimes we come up against barriers that we can't really understand. They don't seem just, right, or well considered ... but sometimes they are there nonetheless. At that point, we go back to the top, and we have those two choices again: fight it, or forget it. A compromise might have been reached, too – you might not completely like the outcome, but your point has been made and you've stood up for what you believe in. Depending on what it is, how exhausted you are, what impact you've made, and whether you can deal with the outcome you've got, don't feel like you've 'lost'. It's also worth remembering that every little bit of effort counts positively. You didn't start out to change the world (you already understood that you, alone, can't stop climate change, can't solve prejudice across the globe and can't stop countries going to war), but you started out to stand up for what's right, for the right reasons. If you've done that, whatever the outcome, you should be proud. Letting go can free your mind from it, while you *know* you've done the right thing, and you *know* you've done a load of good. Don't forget that. Well done, you legend.

5) BE HOPEFUL

Whatever you're facing, and however insignificant your own efforts seem, never lose hope. Just remember: there could be hundreds of thousands of people across the world all doing their little bit – just like you – to push things forward, make things better, and to give a voice to the voiceless. Just because you know you can't change it overnight doesn't mean that it's not worth trying, and trying, and trying again. Don't lose faith and, when things go wrong, don't be downhearted.

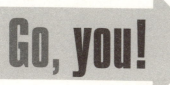

Go, you!

STUCK INSIDE THE PROBLEM

It's one thing trying to help others, but suffering as a result of one of the problems that plague us is something completely different. There are many people who fight against these every day not only because they *want* to support people, but because they *need* to. Let's use free school meals as an example.

Thousands of young people qualify for free lunches at school. It could be to do with parents' income or circumstances at home. Now, it's fantastic that they're provided, and it's absolutely right that they are. But, as we've spoken about, you're only actually at school for about 200 days every year. That means that thousands of people up and down the country – it could be you, reading this right now, or it could be your best friend or your partner in drama – are at home, needing to find meals for 165 other days a year. That's hard for their parents, and could easily leave them pretty hungry. Thankfully, there are charities out there to help. They don't *fix* it – it's linked to inequality in society, how we support those around us and loads to do with the values of a community – but charities and initiatives at least do some good towards shuffling slowly to help those who are living on the edge of the wicked problem itself.

These wicked problems can bring about a real-life psychological toll on others, so we should all do whatever we can to make our mark and to highlight problems when we see them. So when you've lain in bed at night and made the decision to act, don't think that you've done a bad thing. It is important that the microcosm you spend 200 days a year in (your school) knows what your principles (remember, in a previous chapter) are. Standing up for what you think (or *know*) is right is the only way to saw away at the huge forest of wicked problems in the world.

If one person takes one saw, changing the landscape would take forever. If we all take our saws and gently cut away little by little, bit by bit, then the forest might just clear.

Maybe, just maybe, we might be able to see a little bit of light poking through the trees sooner than we think.

THE MARATHON:
HOMEWORK, REVISION, TRAINING, RACING ... AND WAITING

As we all know, secondary school is hard. Grades aren't handed out in a raffle at the end of five years after you've bought a few tickets from your teachers on the way in, and qualifications aren't given for how much money your family earns, for however nice your trainers are, or for how many lovely holidays you've been on. It comes down to your understanding, your knowledge, and your ability to turn up, day in, day out, and learn what you need to learn. It's that hidden hard work that makes all the difference. So, let's look at how we can get through all that work, without getting overwhelmed.

It's actually a bit like running a marathon. And speaking as someone who *has* run a few marathons, there are a few quite wonderful moments. Those include:

SETTING OFF[1]

With the **HAAAARNK** of an air horn and a huge cheer, I was off, and *excited*!

---

[1] Usually at a disgusting hour on a Sunday morning with a belly full of bananas and carbohydrates, but forget that bit.

SEEING A GROUP OF FRIENDS WHO'D TAKEN A TRIP TO WATCH ME WITH A HOME-MADE BANNER AND A BAG OF SUGARY SWEETS

A much-needed boost to make me realise that what I'm doing matters, and that people care!

HITTING THE HALFWAY MILESTONE AND REALISING THAT I *CAN* DO IT

Nearly there. Keep going. I've come so far now – the training's paying off ...

SEEING MY FAMILY AT THE FINISH LINE

The moment that I realise I've finished, I've done it, and I've achieved what I didn't think I could do, even a few hours before, is *wonderful*!

REALISING HOW MUCH GOOD THE CHARITY DONATIONS I COLLECTED WOULD DO

I did this because I wanted to do it, but also to try and do some good. It was an *amazing* moment to see the money I had raised, knowing the brilliant work it would do.

There are, though, also many, many bits that I did not enjoy about the process. Before we link this to school, and your journey through it, let me tell you them:

TRAINING

Sometimes fun (on a sunny day, with a short run, when I actually was 'into it'), but very regularly, a real pain. Often for hours at a time, regularly in darkness, and frequently joined on my runs by sideways rain and wind. Awful at times, but so, so, so important. Without it, the marathon itself is impossible. It would've fallen apart and I would have ended up (at best) not finishing the marathon on the day, or (at worst) injuring myself quite badly.

PAIN

It hurt. Blisters on blisters and walking around school like a pirate grimacing for days and days afterwards. Not much fun.

'Are you okay, sir?'

'No, but thank you for asking!'

The race day itself[2] was *amazing*. And I know exactly why it was. It came down to one thing: preparation.

Had I not prepared, I would have had a dreadful day. I wouldn't have looked forward to it, had those fantastic memories or have been able to say, 'I did it.' The crisp, October afternoon when I crossed the line, wrapped myself in a shimmering silver blanket and felt a huge sense of relief and achievement actually *started* about nine months before.

---

[2] I say 'race', not because I actually wanted to beat anyone, but because that's just what they're called …

The cold evening the previous January, when I'd set off running, lungs burning, feeling like this was an awful idea, but persevering and realising it needed to be done.

But you're not here to tell me about your running exploits, Burton, you clown ...

Fair enough. Good point. Excuse the red nose and big shoes.

So, school, then. That's what we're talking about, isn't it? Well, some of you will have realised why I'm going on about marathons[3] and what the relevance of all this is. It's simple: school is like running a marathon. A long, tough slog ... but definitely worth the hard work.

[3] I promise you it isn't so that you picture me in a vest – I don't want to put you off your evening meal.

The highs of your leaving assembly, the moments you silently clench your fist and let a **'YEESSSSS!'** out to yourself when that assessment you were terrified about in biology goes well, the knowing look you give your friend in the playground when you have an 'in joke', the amazing moments you share with teachers when science experiments go **BANG!** and you jump, the memories of school trips and throwing up on a coach, the pride you feel at parents' evening when you're praised like some kind of idol, the unrivalled joy you feel when you get told about a snow day before you've even got out of bed ... and that surreal moment at the prom where your teacher's wearing a cream tuxedo, a glittery bow tie, and looks very different.

PLAN, PREPARE AND PERSEVERE

Those things don't happen if you do this stuff part-time. You need to be all in. And a *lot* of that is actually done out of the classroom. It's about making sure you stick to your routines and making sure they work for you, to get homework and revision done (and done well), so that you're organised, you're happy, and you have time to do other things too.

That means prioritising things well. What's important, what are your weak spots, and what needs doing *now*? Do that now, and then move on to the next bit. Keep an organised list of what's needed, so that you can put a highly satisfying line through it when it's done. But understand that this stuff is your marathon training – some in the sun which will go amazingly well and flow from your pen onto the page, and some in the sideways rain, uphill, in the dark, on your own, where your sugary sweets have dropped out of your pocket onto the floor three miles ago … and those maths equations will just *not* make sense.

URGENT AND IMPORTANT

- Crisis
- Problems
- Deadlines

IMPORTANT, BUT NOT URGENT

- Opportunites
- Progress
- Long term

URGENT, BUT NOT IMPORTANT

- Maintenance
- Routine tasks

NOT URGENT AND NOT IMPORTANT

- Trivia

It also could mean prioritising your work over what else is out there. There might be a party for your friend's birthday, or a trip out somewhere that you *know*, deep down, is at a time you should be revising. Sometimes, those sacrifices are really important in making sure that you give yourself the very best chance of success. That doesn't mean that you can't have fun, though – of course you can! In the planning part, make sure that you set time aside for things you want to do – like the party everyone will be talking about on Monday morning, or a cinema trip, a night off to watch TV, or even just half an hour staring at your phone and learning a new TikTok dance. There's absolutely no shame in taking time for yourself – it's a really important part of learning – so

build it in, plan for it and enjoy it when it arrives.

WHY IS IT ALL UPHILL? DOES IT EVER STOP?!

There'll be loads of those moments – when the work *just will not make sense at all* – and that's the same for everyone. But if you're up against a hill like that in a marathon, and you just can't run up it, there's no shame in walking. Slow down, ask for help, and people will definitely be able to see that you're working hard, still breathing heavily, and will be more than willing to help. Your maths teacher spending a couple of minutes, rephrasing the way those equations are being taught, is very likely to unlock things in your head. Once you've reached the top of that hill, gulp down another mouthful of water, take a moment to rest, get those trainers back on, and let's get moving again!

GET AHEAD OF THE COMPETITION

To know how the marathon is actually going to go, you need to know how best to train. The best way to know what training to do is to understand the course. Is it uphill or downhill? Is it on grass, sand, gravel, roads or jelly? Preparing for a marathon on the roads of your local town before turning up and finding everyone else is in their trunks and ready for a 26-mile swim suggests you should've planned ahead a bit more.

MOCKS – WHAT TO DO AND WHY ARE THEY IMPORTANT?

As you go through school, you are going to be doing exams. Usually towards the end of secondary school, they might be called 'mocks'. That doesn't mean that you should mock them.[4] Quite the opposite, actually.

Take them seriously.

Find out as early as you can things like when they'll be, which paper will be when, what will be examined, and then start to plan as early as you can for that set of exams.

---

[4] People who say mocking things like 'Haha! I don't need to do these *stupid* things; I think they're pointless!' are rarely as prepared as they should be ...

CRAMMING – NO, NO, NO, NO, NO!

If you'd turned up on marathon morning having just done one HUGE run the day before to train, you would break. You'd be tired, you wouldn't have any stamina built up, and you just would not be ready. It's the same thing for your mock exams. Cramming (revising the night before your exam in a panic because **'AAAARGH, I'VE GOT AN EXAM TOMORROW AND I HAVEN'T DONE ANYTHING FOR IT!'**) doesn't do you any good and certainly doesn't help you to relax.

But how do you avoid cramming when there are so many exams and so little time?

1) GIVE YOURSELF TIME

School will let you know in really good time when they're coming, so as soon as that happens, make a calendar listing when your exams are, and then track-back a schedule to train for them.

2) LIST WHAT YOU NEED TO KNOW

On the list of topics, underline the bits you're struggling with in red, the stuff that's okay in amber, and your strengths in green.

Then you can start to ...

3) PLAN AND PRIORITISE

Target your weaker areas more than the bits you've already got nailed down. Space your revision out so that, rather than going over the same information time after time, you work on different bits every day, revisiting those key bits you struggle with. Slowly but surely, you'll help to move it into your long-term memory.

4) CHUNK IT DOWN!

Don't try to get too much done all at once. It's pretty much impossible, so there's no point trying. Group your topics together so that the things you're covering in that session link together and the knowledge you revise follows a thread which makes sense.

5) TRACK YOUR PROGRESS AND TEST YOURSELF AGAINST LAST WEEK'S QUESTIONS

When you go back to it (use someone at home to quiz you) check how much you've remembered, and make sure it's gone into your brain.

6) CHANGE IT UP!

Revision isn't just reading from a book and making notes. There are trial questions, fact-recall activities, timed quizzes and learning mnemonics to help with tough stuff. There are loads of different things to do to actually get the revision done. The internet, even some of your favourite social media sites, has loads of different helpful resources and past-paper questions ... so find what works for you, and make it yours!

7) DON'T PUSH YOURSELF

Little and often – just half an hour per day to start with (because you're so organised and you've started so early, remember). When you've done your revision, put a really satisfying highlighter line through it, and keep your notes in an organised folder.

8) REWARD YOURSELF

When you've worked hard, you deserve to celebrate it. Don't throw a party every time you learn some quotes for English, but do stop, acknowledge your efforts and do something that makes you smile.

9) WORK IN DAYLIGHT

Working in the hours of darkness, under a light bulb rather than in natural light, can cause headaches, migraines and can eat into your sleep schedule. Wherever you can – and if you have exams in December or January, for example, it might not be - work in a room where there's a window, and position yourself so that the light shines onto you from the front so that the glare from your screen (if you're using one) is reduced and doesn't damage your eyes.

10) FUEL YOURSELF!

Your body needs water and food to keep going. If you're using your brain power to struggle through some really tough stuff, then you're going to need even more of it. Don't feel guilty in breaking for lunch, and keep a glass of water by your side to sip so that you stay awake, keep alert and hydrate your body.

WHEN THE EXAMS ARRIVE . . .

Seeing those exams as a goal to aim for, and train for, little and often, up to the day, takes away the scariness of them. You build up to them, rather than feeling as if you're doing something that you're not ready for.

Focus your revision on your weak spots,

but work on your strong bits too, so you can make the most of those questions. It might be the equivalent of the boring, dark, hard training runs (with the wind and the sideways rain), but the more of those that you do, the easier they get, and the more amazing marathon day will be.[5] And treat yourself to some sweets afterwards. You deserve them.

[5] Apart from the bananas. They're gross. Totally gross.

Planning and preparation, just like routine, aren't seen as the most glamorous things, but they certainly are the most important part of being able to perform on race day. Those who finish those marathons put the time in away from the race and build up stamina so that every time there's an unexpected bump, a bridge they hadn't known about or a change in the course from gravel to thick mud, it really doesn't matter. They've prepared for so long, that there's plenty of stamina, confidence and strength in their lungs and legs.

Pretty soon, you'll be tapering in towards

race day, and you'll be just about ready to go.

Your 'race' is the set of exams at the end of secondary school, and, because you've prepared so well with that hidden, individual revision and those pieces of homework that have helped you to build and build over time, they're going to go really well.

UNDER PRESSURE

Pressure is normal. If you'd not done your training, bought the right trainers and a very fetching vest for your race, then you wouldn't feel the pressure. If you were standing at the start line in a pair of jeans and some flip-flops, wondering how you got there, you wouldn't expect anything of yourself.

Pressure, quite often, comes from expectations, and *really caring* about meeting them. In the exam you might picture telling your grandad about how well it went, or the moment when that brown envelope is torn open and the amazing grades come tumbling out on the page in front of you. But you've got those pictures in your head – those visualisations of what success will look like and feel like – because you *know* you've worked for it. You *know* you can do it.

The night before an exam can be a tough one to crack, too, for the same reason – you care! How should you spend it, and what should you do? Well, lucky for you, I've got five top tips:

1) DON'T CRAM

We've touched on the fact that cramming isn't good before. Just like you wouldn't wait until the rest of your family has one slice of pizza left before you start eating, cramming all eight pieces in within two minutes, you can't revise the whole curriculum the night before. Do a little bit, go over key points, but don't overdo it and stop nice and early.

2) EAT WELL

Make sure you eat at a sensible time, a few hours before you go to bed, so that you're not resting on a full stomach. You're going to need loads of brain power for tomorrow's exam, so good stuff to eat to prepare yourself are things like fish and other seafood which are rich in Omega-3 fatty acids. Vegetables will help, too, as they'll slooooow down digestion and make sure that your energy – from carbohydrates in things like bread, pasta and rice – is released more slowly. That'll mean you've got stamina for tomorrow's battle with biology, and that you'll not need a siesta in the middle of your Spanish writing paper.

3) SENSIBLE BEDTIME

You might be tense and nervous, but keeping to your normal bedtime routine, and getting enough sleep, will help you ahead of tomorrow.

Normal routine, normal processes, normal sleep.

4) NO SCREEN TIME FOR AN HOUR

The blue light that your phone screen kicks out can keep you awake and stop your body relaxing into bedtime. As challenging as it might be, put your phone down and focus on doing something which isn't screen-based. Your eyes need a rest –

they're going to be busy tomorrow!

5) KEEP IT NORMAL

Above all else, these should be normal parts of your routine that's evolved over time. It won't be exactly the same as the one when you first started at secondary school – you might have a later bedtime, and you might have a job for a couple of hours on an evening, for example – but keeping things ticking over as usual and not changing things drastically is important.

RACE TIME!

Once you're up and ready, and have breakfasted well, you're into the exam. A question might well crop up that you're not 100 per cent sure on, and then the pressure might start to create a bit of sweat at the bottom of your back or on your palms, or it might make your heart start to flutter a bit, like you've swallowed a butterfly.

That's fine. Time to reset a moment. Deep breaths, in and out, one to ten.

Then refocus, think again, and do your best. Exam nerves are normal – you feel that way because you care – so follow your revision plan, breathe, visualise what success will look like, and get in there and do it ...

RACING REALITY

The race itself won't be half as bad as you thought, and even though it's actually a challenge and sometimes really, *really* hard (it's supposed to be hard work, or else what would be the point?), you'll enjoy it. You'll storm round that road or track or muddy path or jelly motorway, and, before you know it, you'll be trotting into the last bit, people cheering all around you, a couple of tears starting to form in your eyes, and catching the proud gaze of your support team as you go through the tape and whisper **'YEESSS! I did it!'** Oh, and sweets. There'll be more sweets. That's never a bad thing.

Of course, in a world where we don't know what's coming from one day to the next, uncertainty doesn't help you. You might think that there's no point in carrying on revising or working, because there are bigger issues around us, and you might wonder what difference you doing your homework will make. I get that – I understand why you'd think it, and it can seem a little bit hopeless.

The thing you can do to make sure that circumstances outside your control don't impact on your life any further than they already have done is to get on with what you do best. If you fall out with a friend in the middle of your revision schedule, do your best to just motor on and tick off those subjects. Deal with it later. If your phone's going mad with the latest gossip when you're halfway through a self-portrait that will form a huge part of your art coursework, then finish that portrait, and then go and catch up with it all afterwards.

THE FINISH LINE

The brown envelope you'll get (which doesn't seem much for all the work you put in) isn't a shiny, glittering medal which you can show off to all your pals.

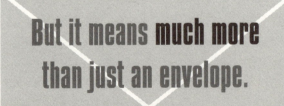

But it means much more than just an envelope.

It's a passport to the next stage of building towards the adult you're going to be. It's proof that, when you train towards a goal, you can achieve it.

Sometimes things go wrong. Can I say that you are *definitely* going to do well, even if you work hard every single day from the age of 11 to 16? Unfortunately not. But in the vast, vast, vast majority of cases, that is exactly what will happen.

Hard work leads to success.

In marathons, in exams, in careers, in sport, in cookery, in flower arranging, in writing, in reading, in *anything in this world*, those who work the hardest tend to benefit from the success that brings.

People do sometimes go against that, though, and there are loads of examples of people who don't do well at school academically who go on to be billionaires and lead amazingly successful companies. Equally, there are many billionaires who have done well at school, have put the training in, set the goals, and done the work (in the same way that you are doing *right now*[6]). They've been sitting at a desk, tired, wishing the exams were over, visualising success (but struggling to believe it'll happen) and getting to race day, quivering, but doing a brilliant job.

[6] Once you've put this book down …

THE WAITING GAME

So, you've finished the race. It was a photo finish. You and the runner next to you appeared to cross at exactly the same time. You're waiting … and waiting … and waiting … and waiting … and …[7] it's tense.

You'll have a while to wait before you find out whether you've achieved what you've been working for. There'll be at least a couple of months to hang on before that moment with the envelope, and the sweaty palms, and the heartbeat that we've talked about before.

No good comes from hanging around just wondering. You've done everything you possibly could have done, and now it's time to celebrate your achievements. Not necessarily the product of those achievements (you obviously don't know what that is yet), but your goal was to get to those exams and do your best. You've absolutely nailed that achievement, so

A MASSIVE WELL DONE!

[7] You get it, you're waiting.

You've gone out there and affected what you actually can affect. That's all you could do. Despite the madness around, the hard miles of training, those moments where it was 9pm at night and it was so ridiculously tough to work out how the gross domestic product of a country is directly linked to its imports in geography. You did all that, and you got there. Well done.

Celebrate your successes, enjoy the fact you have made it to the finish line, and then get ready for the next race, next year. It'll be a different type of race depending on where you go and what you choose to do... but it'll be another one to plan for, prepare for, and slowly but surely move towards that goal. But for now, step away from the books, watch that series on Netflix everyone's been going on about, see your friends, get outside and enjoy the fact you're where you are, having done what you've done. Whatever's in that envelope will still be there in a couple of months, whether you pace up and down your bedroom trying to work out what you wrote, try checking on internet forums what other people put, work out what the grade boundaries might be... or just take some well-deserved time off.

You did it – congratulations! Enjoy it. And have even more sweets. You deserve them, too.

And maybe even an ice cream.

WHERE AM I GOING?

PLANNING A A ROUTE TO

SUCCESS

(AND NOT AN OLD LADY'S BACK GARDEN)

The secondary school journey is weird, isn't it? Blink and you'll miss it, but there are moments, lessons, days, weeks and half-terms along the way that seem to drag on forever. Within what feels like a few breaths it can go from:

1. FEELING MASSIVELY OVERWHELMING

– as you arrive and see all the big kids looking so confident and cool – to ...

2. AMAZINGLY AWESOME

– as you find your feet, make your friends and thrive in your lessons and beyond – and then make a swing to being utterly ...

3. SCARY AGAIN

– as you realise that this isn't 'it' for ever – and there's a whole other world to learn about when you leave.

DECISIONS, DECISIONS, DECISIONS ...

There will come a time when you're going to have to make the first choices about your career. Don't panic – nobody's asking you at 14 to sign a contract for the rest of your life sticking you to a job which you later decide you *really* don't want to do. However, it's a good opportunity, as you start to specialise in a few courses that you're really interested in and/or like, to start to think about what the future might hold.

Choosing your options can be a really difficult point where these three emotions can really smash into each other, leaving you worried, excited and tense all at the same time. While it'll feel like there's a lot of pressure – 'You need to make your choices by Friday the 22nd at 3pm and not a *moment* later, please!' – you don't need to panic.

Calm down.

These are nudges towards the future; you're not setting sail for your final destination. Nobody wants you to – you're only 14! This chapter is all about those choices, what they mean, where they can lead, and how to make them while keeping your options (excuse the pun) open!

SIGNING YOUR LIFE AWAY?

In short:

NO, YOU'RE NOT.

Choices you make about subjects in school are moveable (usually), as long as you act reasonably quickly. You probably won't want to, because you're probably likely to love them. As soon as you start business studies, your teacher will be great, you'll realise you love learning about the world of business and will have already planned how you'll make your first million (and what wonderful holidays you'll spend it on). If, on the other hand, you're knee-deep in business studies after three weeks and can't work out profit from loss and marketing from management structures (and have realised you've made a mistake), then do not fear!

Your teachers, your parents and everyone else around you want you to, above everything else, be happy. If you're not, and if it's a problem for you, then as long as it's changeable they'll do whatever they can. Obviously, if it's a bump in the road and you're well into the course you've chosen before you kick off and decide,

'I HATE BUSINESS STUDIES! AAAAAAGH!'

then that's different; it's about supporting and helping you through.

You are not signing on a dotted line to say you will be a gold prospector, politician or a snake milker by picking an exam option. You're merely specialising in fewer subjects so that you can focus your efforts on doing well in those you like. Think of all the hard work you've put into 12 subjects now being channelled into your favourite eight. It's really important that it's you making those choices, but it's also so important that you talk to (and take the good advice from) your teachers (who've seen good choices and bad choices *many* times before, and will tell you if they think you're making a mistake), but also from your team at home. They might want you to follow in their footsteps and run the 300-year-old family Golf Ball Diving business, but will also understand that you are an individual who needs to make individual choices.

OOH, A SHINY NEW SUBJECT!

There are probably going to be some new and jazzy subjects wafted in front of your nose when you make the choices of the subjects you're going to study as you start the path through your exam years. That'll be because some subjects just aren't studied early on in secondary school. They could be new languages, new vocational subjects[1] and new academic qualifications ... and the chances are that one (or two, or maybe even three) might catch your eye. After all, you've been doing *these old ones* for *years* now: maybe, just maybe, it's time for a change!

Well, be careful. Just because Biblical Hebrew is offered doesn't mean you're quite the right fit for it. A pre-qualification for studying law is not watching a scene in your favourite soap where a dramatic court case happened and someone went to prison for 56 years, screaming, **'NOOOOOOOOOOOOOOOOO! BUT IT WASN'T ME; IT WAS THE GUINEA PIG!'** as they were dragged away by police to spend forever in Her Majesty's Hotel.[2] In the same way you would check whether a cup of tea is **BOILING HOT** and

---

[1] Subjects that are linked specifically to a particular job or profession, like catering, business, textiles, health and social care or construction.
[2] The next week, the guinea pig can't deal with the shame and confesses in a dramatic scene through an interpreter <DER DER DER DU DU DU DUDUDUDU> and the character is freed back to his old life ...

likely to scald you before drinking it, you'd take a sip.[3] Find out what's in it, how suited you are to it, and whether it's genuinely – when you've researched, read and wrestled in your mind – something you want to do. Just because it's new doesn't mean it's for you!

SLOW THINGS DOWN – YOU'RE NOT THAT OLD!

Everyone involved knows that there's a long way to go. It might feel like teachers, parents, grandparents, careers advisors and even the neighbour's cat who once left a dead mouse on your doorstep are all pushing you to choose this pathway, or that course, or the qualification which will set you on a course to that university, but, deep down, everyone (including the cat) knows that you're young, and a lot of things can happen between the day you choose those options and the day you step out as the lead character in a

---

[3] And *please*, I *beg* of you. Not one of those awful, gross, loud sips. Shudder.

West End production of an as-yet-unwritten musical about a friendly cat from next door who had a weird psychological power which it used to encourage 14-year-olds to choose certain subjects for their final exams ...

We've already covered what's important with these choices, but a brief recap wouldn't hurt:

1) MAKE SURE THEY'RE YOUR CHOICES

Your mum and dad might want you to be a doctor or a builder, but they don't dictate your future, and they aren't the ones who have to go to school and study the subjects every day! However, number 2 is also important when I say ...

2) TAKE THE ADVICE OF PEOPLE AROUND YOU SERIOUSLY

It might feel like people are pushing and pulling you this way and that, but you should listen to them; they've done this stuff and they

only want the best for you.

3) REMEMBER YOU HAVE TO ENJOY THEM!

You have to do the hard work of studying, learning, completing class work and homework in these subjects for the next few years, so

MAKE SURE YOU CAN GET ALONG WITH THEM!

Think of the subjects as if you're going to be on a loooooong car journey with them: will you have enough to talk about, or are they going to drive you crazy?

4) KEEP THEM BROAD!

Not many people at 14 know exactly what the next five years will look like, let alone the next 50. Most people don't retire until they are in their sixties (and that's a *lot* of years away). The world is going to look really different then, but, more importantly, *you* are going to be (and look) very different too! Keep those qualifications and subjects nice and broad, so that lots and lots of different pathways are open to you later, whether that's college, work, apprenticeship, university or anything else.

GAZING INTO THE CRYSTAL BALL . . .

When you're plotting your path, it's also an important thing to consider where the path actually leads. We've all taken a wrong turning on a country walk before, and ended up in a bemused old lady's back garden, before apologising and turning back, blaming each other for the mistake. Well, we don't want your qualifications to lead you to somewhere that you don't want to be.

You want to avoid doing subjects which count each other out (school will make sure that doesn't happen), you want to avoid doing ones which are too narrow and don't let you change your mind (because your mind, almost definitely, will change), and you want them to cover lots of interesting, engaging, tough, challenging work. The end result will be grades that accelerate your path to the next stage, and we all want that to be the top of the hill with a wonderful view over your future, at college, sixth form, work or an apprenticeship (and not behind the shed in an old lady's garden with a view of her washing, some cracked paving stones and a shattered, ageing greenhouse).

YOUR LIFE IS YOURS:
LIVE IT
AND
LOVE IT!

10

Why the **tough** days, the **meh** mornings, and the **crazy chemicals** are worth it in the end

So here we are, nearly at the end.[1] COVID-19 hasn't made your path through secondary school any easier. In fact, it has probably made it a lot more challenging, whether it started for you back in primary, or interrupted your first few months at secondary. Not that you're complaining, I know. You're resilient.

But know this:

you're here, and **YOU** made it.

You live in a world where you can embrace, talk, meet, high-five, fist-bump, handshake, hold each other and, above all, be together. Because that's what makes humans, human; it's what makes schools, schools.

---

[1] You must be absolutely inconsolable. I'm sorry, but there's only so much paper before the trees run out.

People.
Principles.
Processes.

We've all *had* to adapt, be brave, and be calm – there has been no choice – but we all hope we won't need to do quite as much of that in the future. We all want the corridors full of people, the classrooms full of hands up, teachers marking your work over your shoulder, exams going ahead as normal and brown envelopes full of grades grabbed by expectant, nervous hands.

Your days at school will always be times that you remember. Whatever you become, however you spend your life, whomever you meet and wherever life takes you, one thing that unites everyone is their time at school. The memories of primary school that people have tend to be a little bit foggy at the edges as time passes by and things fade, but the big difference in secondary school is that the older you get, the more recent it is, the more conscious of everything you are, so the more you remember.

That will mean many different things for many different people. Some people have really good experiences and will look back with a smile plastered across their face. Things went well, they had good friends, they made good choices and they left with what they needed to make the leap to the next 'bit'. They'll look back and reminisce[2] with friends they've kept for years to come, and always think fondly of their time there.

Lovely, if that's your experience.

Unfortunately, that won't be everyone. And if you're in the middle of it now, and that's definitely *not* your experience, you're not forgotten, and you're not on your own. This book isn't excluding you, and it isn't trying to put a shimmer and shine on the fact that, for some people, this is true: school can be a real grind, and has been in recent times for more people than ever before.

Either way, though, believe me: your experience is *your* experience. Whether it's your mum, your dad, your teachers, your grandparents, your guardians, your friends, some teacher chap from Yorkshire who's written a book,[3] nobody

---

[2] Share stories (usually lovely, funny and all-round good) and memories, before leaning back into a comfortable chair and saying something like, 'Aaaaaaahhhhh, good times …' while staring into the distance with a medium-sized smile on their face.
[3] That's me, in case you didn't get it. Oh, you did. Sorry. Ignore this then.

can tell you how to feel. They can help, guide and advise you, but they can't *tell* you or *force* you ... and that, in particular, is what makes secondary school both wonderful and terrifying in equal measure.

You're going to be overcome with emotions at times for reasons you can't control (your body is going to do that to you, as are the events we're living through), and you're going to feel completely overworked and overwhelmed at times (again, because it's hard and tough and you'll need to work for what you want), but that doesn't mean that you can't do it.

No, no, no, no, no, NO! You, my friend, *can.* 100 per cent you *can.*

Are you going to get top grades in everything all the time? No. And don't expect yourself to. If you do, then treat it as a lovely surprise.[4] But expecting full marks in everything is superhuman, and even superheroes have the odd off day.

School is an amazing journey,

and you are going to have a few years that you will never forget. You will have moments that are etched in your mind forever and will always make you smile in memory of when they happened – the people, the smells, the surroundings will all come flooding back, even when you're old and telling your grandchildren's children's goldfish about them.[5]

[4] And you do have a VERY GOOD CHANCE of doing it if you work incredibly hard!
[5] Not because talking to goldfish is going to become something that people do in the future ... but because you'll have talked about it so much to everyone else that the only living being who'll listen is the one who forgets things as quickly as you've told them.

But between now and then, when those tiny little goldfish are staring up at you from their bowl, one or two things are going to go wrong. You will, at some stage, feel like the world is burning down around you and you won't know what to do. But you do know, really. You've got this...

Always, always, always remember that...

1) ... YOU ARE STRONGER THAN YOU THINK

You have got through things before, and you'll do it again. Hold firm to what you know, and plan your way out.

2) ... YOU ARE IN COMMAND OF YOUR CHOICES

However you've ended up here, whether through bad choices or bad fortune, the next decision you make is yours. Plan for it being a good one – the right one – and you'll soon see things moving.

3) . . . NOBODY CAN TAKE YOUR HOPE AWAY

However bad things get, your hope and your plans and your expectations of yourself are yours. They're not anyone else's to have.

The power of hope is HUGE.

Never give it up, and remember that you are allowed to hope, pray and wish.

4) ... WHATEVER'S GOING ON, YOU CAN STILL BE POLITE

Please. Thank you. Holding doors. Smile. People will remember that. Treat people how you would want to be treated.

5) ... YOU HAVE A RIGHT TO SPEAK THE TRUTH

If someone has put you in a tough spot, then be honest about it and speak out. Your life is yours, and you deserve to live it how you want to. The truth can set you free.

If you think of plotting your experiences on a graph, wonderful days being a 10, and those rubbish days that we all have being a 1, then what do you think would be a good average to aim for? I reckon probably about an 8. So, let's resolve that we're going to aim for 8 out of 10 on average,

shall we? If we can consistently smash out an 8 out of 10 –
allowing for loads to be amazing and so many wonderful
memories to be created – then you'll do fabulously well, and
you'll have a supersonic time at school.

We can't forget what's happened, and we shouldn't. We
owe it to everyone around us not to. Every single person on
the face of this planet will be carrying different baggage to
what they were before the COVID-19 pandemic started and,
whether you look to the future with hope or despair, that
future *will* still arrive. So let's do it together with hope. Let's
do everything we can, which comes down to the basics:
working hard, and being nice.

Yes, let's do that, shall we? Let's not let this dreadful virus
take a single thing more than it already has from us all.

Let's get Back on Track.

RESOU

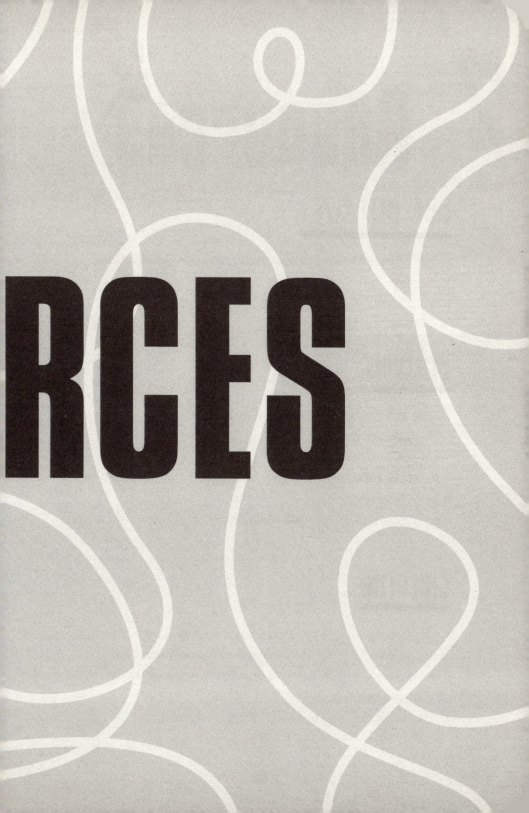

Resources

BBC BITESIZE

A free online resource to help with homework, revision and learning.
https://www.bbc.co.uk/bitesize

BULLYING

Online advice on bullying and mental health.
https://www.bullying.co.uk

Lots of information on bullying, including cyberbullying, and how to deal with it.
http://www.anti-bullyingalliance.org.uk/

CHILDLINE

A counselling service for children and young people. Their website has lots of advice, articles, games and message boards on everything from mental health and money, to school and bullying.
https://www.childline.org.uk

MIND

Mind is a mental health charity. In the link below you can find information about mental health, well-being and how to find support.
https://www.mind.org.uk/information-support/for-young-people/

SEXUALITY

Practical advice and support for children coming out as LGBT. Also includes a useful search function for support and communities local to your area.
https://www.youngstonewall.org.uk/